How to Start an Online Bakery from Home

Create Profitable Baked Goods on Your Own Terms.

Madaline Hart

© Copyright 2022 - All rights reserved.

The content contained within this book may not be reproduced, duplicated or transmitted without direct written permission from the author or the publisher.

Under no circumstances will any blame or legal responsibility be held against the publisher, or author, for any damages, reparation, or monetary loss due to the information contained within this book, either directly or indirectly.

Legal Notice:

This book is copyright protected. It is only for personal use. You cannot amend, distribute, sell, use, quote or paraphrase any part, or the content within this book, without the consent of the author or publisher.

Disclaimer Notice:

Please note the information contained within this document is for educational and entertainment purposes only. All effort has been executed to present accurate, up to date, reliable, complete information. No warranties of any kind are declared or implied. Readers acknowledge that the author is not engaged in the rendering of legal, financial, medical or professional advice. The content within this book has been derived from various sources. Please consult a licensed professional before attempting any techniques outlined in this book.

By reading this document, the reader agrees that under no circumstances is the author responsible for any losses, direct or indirect, that are incurred as a result of the use of the information contained within this document, including, but not limited to, errors, omissions, or inaccuracies.

Table of Contents

Introduction

The bakery business is one of the fastest growing businesses in America. This is because of the increased consumption of bakery products and the ease of starting a bakery, compared to other kinds of businesses. In truth, starting a business is a big step and it requires an entrepreneurial mindset to run it successfully. Starting a business begins with conditioning your mind to have a healthy mindset and take control of your decisions. What are the current business beliefs holding you back and how can you overcome them to build a healthy mindset to maintain a successful bakery business?

If you are interested in starting an online bakery from home, but the idea seems ambiguous and you don't know where to start from, this is the right book for you. It doesn't matter if you don't have any ideas about running a bakery. Every single step that is involved in starting an online bakery from home is broken down in this book. It begins with guiding you through writing a thorough business plan for your bakery which includes your business goals and description, product description, and marketing, operational and financial plans. The book will go on to explain the equipment needed for your startup bakery and their prices, important baking tips needed to bake delicious products, a breakdown of steps to creating a business entity suitable for your business and the important laws and regulations concerning starting a home bakery. One of the major challenges business owners face is to come up with the right strategies to price their products to ensure that substantial profit is made. Reading this book will subdue the fear of this challenge and give a clear knowledge on how to price your products. Promoting your business to attract and increase sales, and getting your goods to customers are very important parts of running a business, and are not left out. Good customer service is also essential to retaining customers and will also be adequately discussed. If all the boxes are ticked and all the steps are followed, your business is expected to grow, so this book also prepares you to plan ahead for scaling.

As you can see, what you have here is the full package, and that is the intention of this book. At the end of the book, you should get sufficient knowledge to make you confident enough to start your online bakery business from home.

Chapter One: You Must Think This Way If You Want to Succeed

People say things like: "Experience is the best teacher, and "Start anyway. You learn on the job." While these statements are not necessarily wrong, a lot of business errors and crises could have been avoided if certain important knowledge was acquired before the business was started. Of course, it is necessary to distinguish between taking the right steps to acquire knowledge for your business, and stalling due to fear of failure. As much as it is advised to take risks, it is also crucial to do so wisely.

Before starting a business, it is important to have the right mindset. Byron Katie said, "Every time your mind shifts, your world shifts," (Katie, 2018). In essence, your mind has great control over the outcome of your decisions. You can achieve whatever you set your mind to. So, a healthy mindset leads to a healthy business. Having the right mindset can keep you going even in the midst of a business crisis.

Some Business Beliefs That Hold Starters Back

Lack Of Personal Life

When people compare businesses with 9-5 jobs, there is a popular notion that entrepreneurs or business owners work round the clock, to the point where they do not have personal lives. People believe that jobs have time limits, as opposed to businesses where you have to respond to customers' requests at whatever time they come. Because of this, business owners work continually, which makes them have little or no time for any other substantial activity. This belief can discourage people who want to start businesses, especially those who value their personal time and also want to have time for family and other activities.

While businesses are time-consuming, and business owners need a great level of commitment to get effective and desired productivity, the fortunate advantage of being a business owner and being your own boss is that you get to set the course of your ship. Owning a business comes with a compulsory time management demand. Managing your time will help you handle your business properly and also create time for other important activities. Having a time based work routine is not limited to only 9 -5 jobs. As a business owner, you can create a work routine that can help you monitor your work schedule, so as to effectively manage your time. So, contrary to popular belief, business owners, who master time management skills, have personal lives.

Business Owners Have To Move With The Trend

While it is important to evolve, it is advisable to move with every trend that comes up. The backbone of any business is its uniqueness. People jump on trends to increase visibility, but you can evolve with trends, without having to change your originality. It is now easier to promote your business, via the internet and different social media, to your potential audience, so you are not obligated to jump on every trend. This mindset can discourage people who are not always trend friendly. As a business owner, before adopting a trend, analyze its relevance to your business, its plan, purpose, and authenticity. At the end of the day, customers will stick with brands that stand out and have a unique identity.

Your Business Idea Must Be Perfect Before Starting Out

When launching a business, it is easy to want to tick all the boxes and bring out the best. It is worse for perfectionists who would rather present a "perfect" business or not start out at all. This mindset has kept a lot of people sitting on their ideas, reluctant to take a step. Your business can never be perfect at its inception. It is necessary to acquire the right knowledge for a business, in order to avoid mistakes, but in a business, you must keep learning on the job. Feedback from your target audience is necessary to keep improving on business. Reid Hoffman, LinkedIn founder said, "If you are not embarrassed by your first product release, you released too late." Despite LinkedIn's rough beginning, Microsoft ended up acquiring the company for $26.2 billion, (Miller, 2018). If you want to be perfect, or you use your initial ideas to judge the future of your business, you will never start.

Reserved People Cannot Market

This is another belief that holds people back from starting a business. Reserved people are believed to lack marketing skills, due to an inability to go out and have conversations with people. As a reserved person, you can see this belief and get automatically discouraged from putting your business ideas out. Does owning a business require you to speak with people? Yes, it does. But you just need to sacrifice your comfort zone and go out of your way to market your products or services. You do not have to be an outgoing person to do that. You can learn conversation, communication and presentation skills, learn to introduce yourself, and speak in front of people. You can also learn marketing skills and keep adding value to yourself so that you can build a niche for yourself and be an inspiration to others.

Businesses With The Greatest Risk Have The Most Success

Some businesses require huge capital and investments to start properly, while some others require patience, commitment and consistency. You need to discover what category your business falls under before taking any steps. Some entrepreneurs have gone into huge debts for businesses that ended up crashing. This mindset can keep people from starting their businesses because it is not high risk. The level of your business risk does not determine how serious your business is, or how successful it will be. The business space has evolved to a point where you can "build on the way." You can start your business from home while, at the same time, finding and meeting investors, and building your customer base. The point is, there is more to starting a business than taking risk, and high risk does not automatically guarantee success

Maintaining a Successful Business

Having the right mindset towards entrepreneurship is important. It is what gives you the boldness to establish yourself in the manner you want to. When your mindset improves, your business improves too. According to Alistair Emerson and his contributors, the most important principle a business owner must possess is an entrepreneurial mindset, (Emerson et al. 2011). This entrepreneurial mindset is defined by Dhliwayo and Van Vuuren as a means of business perception and its opportunities in a manner that usurps uncertainty, (Dhliwayo and Van Vuuren, 2007). In essence, the probability of a business succeeding or failing is dependent on the presence or absence of the entrepreneurial mindset in the business owner. The entrepreneurial mindset can be characterised by:

- The enthusiasm to find opportunities by being on the lookout for new trends in your business niche and going after these opportunities in a tactical, prompt and right manner.

- The ability to implement changes properly.

- Being disciplined enough to discern the right timing.

- Being open minded enough to explore different means of execution, depending on which is best, (McGrath and MacMilan 2012).

As it has been explained, having an entrepreneurial mindset is very essential in building and maintaining a successful owner business.

Mindset to Develop in Order to Build and Maintain a Successful Business

- Being Goal Oriented:

You cannot start a business without a business idea and goals. The reason we set goals is so that we can monitor our actions and progress as individuals, or as a business. Business owners with the entrepreneurial mindset are not just wishers, but goal setters. This is why a business plan is very important. Building and maintaining a successful business requires you to set specific, measurable, attainable, relevant and time sensitive (SMART) goals.

- Being Action Driven:

If you are not action driven, your business ideas will not take shape. As a business owner, you should be prompt in your actions, and avoid stalling. Stalling can make you miss out on several opportunities and the timing of important changes to be made. Entrepreneurs are not just talkers, but doers. To develop a successful business, you need to take the necessary steps towards achieving desired results. Lynch et al. carried out research by collecting a total of 51 interviews from different successful companies, and the word "build" was mentioned 230 times, (Lynch et al. n.d.). You cannot build, nor be successful if you do not take action.

- Having Problem Solving Ideas:

A business that will be relevant, attract customers and keep them coming back is a business that solves a problem. Good business ideas are constructed from seeking to solve a discovered problem. For instance, ride hailing companies make transportation easier and more comfortable. Companies like Zoom and Skype solve the problem of meeting limitations due to distance, by creating a platform for people to have meetings from all parts of the world. For companies like that, their target audience will keep increasing because they solve a crucial problem and meet customers' needs. Before starting a business, ask yourself, "What problem is this solving?" Remember that your business is as relevant as the problem it solves.

- Being Future Minded:

Successful business owners are focused more on the future than the past. They understand that it is impossible to change the past, while you still have opportunities to grow, effect desirable changes and seize chances in the future. A successful business requires you to be a forward thinker.

- Customer Sensitivity:

A business owner who is particular about building a successful business must be sensitive to and understand customers' wants, needs and satisfaction. This mindset helps you to focus on your customers' success, which thereby influences your business' success. This creates a win-win situation, helps your business grow, and makes you an authority in your niche.

- Taking Responsibility:

A business owner with an entrepreneurial mindset is willing to take full responsibility for whatever happens in the business. A characteristic of successful business owners is that they do not blame others for circumstances, even if it was not their fault. Taking responsibility empowers you to take charge of the situation and make necessary changes. The entrepreneurial mindset is a no-excuse zone.

- Create a Crisis management Plan:

Some crises are predicted, while some are not. One way to ensure the success of your business is to create a crisis management plan. Many businesses are severely affected during a crisis due to lack of adequate planning. Planning for future crises does not translate to being negative; it only prevents unpreparedness. During the start of your business, you can create a list of possible disasters that can occur over time, and coinciding adequate solutions. An example of a company that has successfully managed a crisis is Pepsi. They were accused of having syringes in the cans of their products in the early nineties. They ran public relations campaigns to debunk and address the allegation and released videos of their actual production process, (PKF Muller, 2016). Pepsi is still a strong company to this day.

- Be Open Minded and Flexible:

Innovation keeps evolving. So, for your business to stand the test of time during a crisis, you must be willing to evolve with the seasons. During the Covid'19 pandemic, many businesses saw the importance of having an online presence, since there was a lockdown around the world. Rigidity is one way to kill your business during a crisis.

Businesses that refused to adapt into the online space suffered losses and found it difficult to rebuild after the pandemic. So, while it is essential to follow your business plan and structure, you should be flexible enough to make changes when needed.

Chapter Two: Mapping Out Your Game Plan

In the previous chapter, the importance of having an entrepreneurial mindset was emphasised. One of the characteristics of an entrepreneur mindset is being goal oriented. Launching a business involves a great deal of preparation and meticulous planning. Proper realistic goals should be set with a monitored time frame and a business plan should be mapped out. Mapping out a business plan takes a lot of effort. Every detail is important, as it gives clarity to future investors. There are also ethical and legal rules to put into consideration. A business plan is the blueprint of your business. It is the foundation which your business ideas are built on. It also helps you to direct your ideas to the right area. It brings your business to life.

Writing A Thorough Business Plan For The Bakery

A well constructed business plan not only convinces future investors to invest in your business, it also encourages your future partner and employees to see your vision and join your company. It also gives you the opportunity to sit down and go through your business ideas, the customer problems you are solving, and the key reasons for starting the business. Then, you can plan out every step, draw up a roadmap that will guide the growth of your business, and prepare your business for success. It also gives you the opportunity to identify the strengths and weaknesses in your business idea, discover prospective investors, identify potential challenges, figure out solutions to potential problems and organize a crisis management strategy.

A sound business plan should be simple and easy to understand, especially by anyone outside your company. Thorough research should be put into writing your business plan and sources researched should be credible. Also, your plan should be time bound and realistic enough for investors and loan organizations to believe in what you are projecting.

The first page of your business plan should contain the date, your company name, street addresses, city, state, ZIP, business phone, website URL (if available) and email address. Then, a confidentiality agreement should be drafted, such that the undersigned reader would agree not to disclose any information supplied by the business plan, except information that is proved to be already public knowledge. The confidentiality agreement should contain a section for the signature, name of the reader and date.

An example is shown below:

Confidentiality Agreement

The undersigned reader agrees that any information supplied by

_________________________________ *in this business plan, except information that is proved to be public knowledge, is confidential. Any disclosure or use by the reader may cause grave damage or harm to*

_________________________________. *Hence, the undersigned reader acknowledges not to share it without clear written approval from*

_________________________________.

Upon request, the undersigned will promptly return this document to

_________________________________.

____

Signature

____

Name

____

Date

This is a business plan. It does not connote an offering of securities.

Executive Summary

An executive summary is the first section that your reader, potential investor or lender/loan organization reads. It states how sound your business plan is and makes them decide whether or not it is worth reading. Though your executive summary comes first, it should be written after the entire business plan has been drawn up, so as to have a well written summary.

The executive summary should concisely state;

•	The summary of your business idea in a few lines.

•	Time bound goals for your business. What is the five year, 7 year and 10 year plan?

•	A proper description of your product or service. What customer needs are you meeting?

- Your potential target customers.

- Your key competitors and unique features. Who are you up against? What makes your business special? What distinct features will separate you from your competitors and give you a competitive advantage?

- Your financial plan for the business. If you are applying for a loan, how much do you need? What is your spending and pricing strategy, and how do you intend to make profit?

After reading your executive summary, your reader should be able to understand the potency of your business and be enthusiastic enough to read further.

Company Description

This section of your business plan should include the company vision, mission statement, goals, industry and legal structure.

Company Vision and Mission Statement

A company vision refers to the values your business stands by. It should state the long term philosophy of your business. What do you want your business to become? What impression do you want it to leave? A mission statement is a brief statement of what your business does or the reason for its existence. It can be a full statement or a tagline/slogan.

Company Goals

This should include your long and short term goals. Your goals should have a timeframe and a standard to measure the growth of your business.

Industry

Describe your industry and your niche. How relevant is the industry? If it is not, what is its growth level and how do you intend to make your business survive? What competitors are you likely to encounter? How do you intend to stand out and develop a competitive advantage?

Legal Structure/Ownership

Is your business a sole proprietorship, LLC, partnership or corporation? What is the motive of choosing that form of business?

Product Description

According to Philip Kotler, a product is a coalition of goods and services a company renders to a particular target audience, (Kotler, 2008). There are three tiers of a product. The first is the manufactured goods or rendered services. After production, your raw product will not find its target market without visibility, no matter the quality. This is where the second tier comes in. With the right branding, design and packaging, your product or service will stand out in your target market, differentiate your business from your competitors, and leave an impression in the minds of your customers. The success of the second tier of your product is dependent on target market and key competitors research, promotion of the specific problems being solved and promotion of the customers needs being met. Competitor advantage in marketing is created by the uniqueness of the value being offered and the distinctiveness of the essential features of your product, in comparison to your key competitors. This creates an appealing image and helps to establish your product in your target market. The last tier includes after sales services like delivery, warranty/guarantee, service contracts, ongoing support, training and refund policy, (Leppävaara, 2015). Basically, these three tiers are important in your product description, as they leave a solid impression in the minds of your customers. Imagine having a quality raw product, but poor packaging or branding. This can affect your customer base, as the first contact they will make with your product is the branding. Let's also say you have a good product and branding, but poor delivery service. That already counts as a bad review. So, the final product you present to your target is a combination of these tiers, and equal efforts should be put into them to give you a competitive advantage.

This section should describe products you are selling or services you are rendering. How do you intend to manufacture them? Explain your products in relation to the problems they are solving or the customer needs they meet. Explain how your product is better than similar products in your target market. Describe the benefits and unique features that give you a competitive advantage. Also, explain how your pricing strategy will affect entire customers and fit into the competitive marketplace. What is your expected profit margin? Also include specifications and other assisting information.

Marketing Plan

This plan explains your target market research, competition research, pricing and distribution strategies, design and advertising strategies and SWOT analysis.

Target Market Research

A target market or audience is a group of customers who demand, buy and consume your business' products or services. This section of your business plan should describe the overall size and current trends of your target market. Explain the growth of your target market and how likely the trends are to change within a specified number of years. This can be done by personal research; by getting credible information from the internet and carrying out surveys on perceived target customers. It can also be done secondarily by getting information from verified sources like journals, magazines, newspapers, trade organizations data, demographic profiles and census data from government agencies.

Target Customer Research

Describe your ideal target customer group and create a demographic profile that should include age, gender, occupation, location, income size, etc. If you intend to deal with businesses, create a profile that should include size, industry, location, business stage, potential annual sales and income size.

Competitor Research

Every business has competition. Apart from understanding your target market, it is important to also identify and study your key competitors, understand how they appeal to their customers, their kind of products or services, distribution channels, and come up with strategies to meet customers needs and wants better. It is essential to develop competitive marketing schemes that can work in your favour and keep you at the greatest possible competitor advantage. Study their motivations, strengths, weaknesses, strategies, and modes of operation, (Kotler and Armstrong, 2008).

SWOT Analysis

Describe your company's strengths and weaknesses. Study your products/services, branding, marketing plan, staff, finance operations, competition status and management strategies to identify them. Can your strength cover up for your weaknesses? After identifying them, what are your proposed steps to improve on them. Identify possible barriers you might encounter during the establishment of your business like, high startup, production and marketing costs, employing qualified staff, brand visibility, etc. Set plans in place to overcome them. Identify the future threats and opportunities you might encounter during the progression of your business like, changes in industry trends, inflation or change in economy, change in government policies and regulations, and change in relevant technology. What is the magnitude of the effect on your business? How do you plan to manage encountered threats?

Pricing Strategy

The price of your products is the most fundamental marketing mix due to the fact that it is the only element that brings direct revenue to your business. The factors that determine the price of a product are cost of production, consumer insight of value, and other pricing factors. A company's cost is constituted of two major forms; the fixed and variable costs. Fixed costs are constant expenses that depend on time and are independent of production or sales quantity. Examples are rent, electricity, lease costs, salaries, insurance, utility bills, etc. Variable costs, on the other hand, are volatile expenses that are dependent on the quantity of production and sales. Examples are costs of raw materials, delivery fee, packaging activities, commission, etc. These costs directly influence a business' pricing strategy. For the consumer insight of value, value based pricing should be employed in order to set a price that represents the value of the product. This can be done by target market research to find out how much your consumers are willing to pay for that particular product. "A product value is created when the benefits a consumer enjoys is greater than the long term costs the customer is willing to pay for a product," (Slater and Narver, 2000). Other factors that can affect pricing strategy are competitors' price and presentations, economy, nature of market, government actions, demand, and other environmental factors (Leppävaara, 2015). All of these should be put into consideration to develop a suitable pricing strategy for your products.

Distribution Strategy

This strategy involves activities that convey the finished products to the target market. Distribution strategies are built and improved by having an updated functional marketing channel. This requires building long lasting relationships with employees, suppliers and customers via proper communication and transactions. According to Kotler, a marketing channel is a channel in which a set of mutually dependent establishments work together to ensure the final product or service is available to the end consumer, (Kotler, 2008). As the marketing channel is crucial in your business' distribution strategy, it is important to select the most appropriate channel. During the selection of a marketing channel, it is of great importance to study factors like the product attributes, market conditions, number of channel members and other environmental factors. The product's attributes include the size of the product; whether small or large, the cost, expensive or cheap, and other attributes, like whether the product is perishable, hazardous, etc. The market condition includes whether the customers are centralised or discharged in your target market. The right number of channel members is considered, whether exclusive, consisting of only one retailer and wholesaler, selective, consisting of a small number of channel members, or inclusive, consisting of as many retailers and wholesalers as possible.

What method will you use to sell your product? Direct sales, ecommerce, retail, wholesale, sales representatives or referrals? Explain the effectiveness and your reasons for choosing the method(s). This should also depend on geographical proximity, staff size, market demand and competitors' positioning.

Marketing and Advertising Strategies

What relevant and influential advertising tactic do you intend to use? Advertising may involve television, radio, online, print etc. Promotional tactics may include content marketing, search engine optimisation (SEO), social media promotion, email marketing, networking etc. All these will depend on the image you want to communicate for your brand. Map out your design brochures, logo, brand materials, etc and insert the marketing budget.

Operational Plan

This should include daily operations, inventory, staff size, production methods or processes, equipment to be used, quality control operations, location and location size, proximity and accessibility to target market, maintenance and utility.

Financial Plan

Developing a detailed financial plan helps you to set realistic financial goals for your business. It also informs future investors or loan organizations that you know what you are doing.

Your financial plan should include startup expenses and capital to describe how much is needed to launch your business, time bound profit and loss projections (one or two years), cash flow projections to track how much your business has at a given moment, balance sheet projection to reveal the business's equity, sales volume projections and proposed use of capital.

Chapter Three: Supplies Needed To Get Started

In starting a bakery business, there are necessary pieces of equipment and supplies you will need. Knowing about the necessary equipment and supplies is important because the cost is to be included in your financial plan, while drawing up your business plan. It also ensures you don't leave out any essential equipment while drawing up the costs. The purpose of this chapter is to enlighten you on the basic equipment and supplies that are necessary to start up your home bakery and to give you an estimated price for this equipment. Having the best equipment suitable for your business will make production easy and help you produce quality products.

Baking Equipment

Below is a list of essential baking equipment needed to run a home bakery.

- Oven:

Without an oven, commercial baking is not executable. The oven is used to heat up the dough after proper mixing. While choosing an oven, the first thing to consider is whether you want an electric or gas oven. You will need a reliable brand that heats properly and is airtight. Convection ovens are one of the most popular types of commercial ovens because they are fast and bake different products evenly; from cakes to bread, brownies, pies and cookies. Of the types of ovens used in a commercial bakery, convection ovens are the least expensive. Deck ovens are preferred by bakers that make particular kinds of bread loaves. They give the bread crust a distinctive crispy feel. Even though deck ovens take up space, they have high durability and last longer than most types of ovens. There are single and double deck ovens. Commercial convection ovens can be gotten within the range of $250 - $1000. Single deck ovens, either electric or gas, are within the range of $100 - $750, while double deck ovens are within the range of $850 - $1400.

- Mixer:

It is more effective to go for a commercial mixer that has a variety of mixing accessories. A stand mixer and hand mixer are time saving and are suitable for a startup online home bakery. A stand mixer can vary around $200 - $1000, depending on your preference, needs, and burden of production.

- Proof boxes for bread items:

Bakery products that utilize yeast need to rise properly. A proof box is a humidity and temperature-optimised environment to enable the dough to rise efficiently. You can also improvise with your oven at the start of your business, if you are trying to cut costs, but it is easier to monitor the rise of the bakery product, at the right temperature, using a proof box. Proof boxes come in different sizes, ranges, capacities and prices. During your research, find the one that suits your budget and expectation. Proof boxes for a home bakery cost between $30 - $200.

- Heavy duty food processor:

A Food processor helps you handle heavy duty processes, and saves time that should be used for other things. It can crush nuts, shave chocolates, and do other tedious processes. If you prefer to do things the old-fashioned way, you can skip this, but it is recommended, since it saves a great deal of your time. Heavy duty food processors can be found within the range of $90 - $500

- Slicer:

If bread is one of your major products, then this piece of equipment is a necessity. It helps you slice the bread into uniform sizes and saves time due to its speed and consistency. Home bread slicers go for $10 - $45, while factory electric slicers cost between $200 - $500.

- Digital kitchen scale:

One thing that bakers often overlook is precision and consistency. A customer should be able to have the same experience each time they order the same cake from you. There was a reason why your cake tasted differently from others, and most times, your secret is from your measurements. If you are not consistent with them, you risk losing your unique taste, thereby losing customers. If you want your customers to keep coming back, you need to be accurate in your measurements. While cups can be used to measure, the weight of standard measuring cups are not always consistent.

For example, you might want to measure 5 cups of flour (150 grams each), making 750 grams, but you get a measuring cup that is 155 grams. This will make you unknowingly measure 25 grams extra.

This can affect the result of your baking process, as every gram of flour is significant.

Because of this, it is important to invest in a digital kitchen scale, for the sake of your business and your customers' satisfaction. Digital kitchen scales do not cost that much and will work to give you your desired result.

Another advantage of using digital kitchen scales is that it makes mixing batter much faster. You can weigh each ingredient into your bowl, obtain the weight, press the zero button and weigh the next ingredient into the bowl. This way, it saves a lot of time and washing up since you will end up using only the mixing bowl, (Lambrechts, n.d.). You can get a digital kitchen scale for $10 - $20.

- Collection of baking pans:

You should have different pans for pies, bread, cakes, cupcakes, etc. You also need to research the different types of pans to know which type suits your business. Getting pans in large quantities, depending on the size of your startup, is cheaper and advantageous. You will also need different sizes of pans and baking sheets. You can start with a small number, and increase the number as the need arises. Bakeware sets of 5 - 7 pans can be bought within the range of $35 - $70.

- Sinks and work table:

Sinks are extremely important for tidying up, keeping your equipment clean and your work environment hygienic. Since you are setting up a home bakery, the sink in your kitchen would be of great use. If you do not have a work table, then there is no platform for work to be done. A work table is needed to carry out the mixing, rolling and cutting of dough, kneading, flouring and other pre-baking processes, before the dough goes into the oven. Invest in a strong and durable work table if you want it to last longer, since a lot of work is going to be done on it, (LaMarco, 2019). A durable work table can cost around $100 - $200.

- Other utensils:

Other utensils needed for a home bakery are spatulas, knives, pots, sifters, dough cutters, stirring spoons, measuring cups, piping bags, a rolling pin, cutting boards, mixing bowls, icing grates, cooling racks, cake stands, whisks, cake boxes, decorating tubes, containers, cake decor utensils and accessories.

Storage Equipment and Supplies

Baking ingredients, supplies and materials need to be stored in a suitable and hygienic environment. The essential storage equipment needed are listed below:

- Refrigerator and freezer:

A good number of your baking ingredients will need to be refrigerated to keep them fresh before use. It also makes your production a lot easier, especially when you have to buy ingredients in bulk. You will be able to store them and handle incoming orders quickly, rather than shopping too frequently. Eggs, cream and milk are ingredients that need to be stored in the refrigerator, to prevent spoilage. You can always use your home refrigerator to store your baking ingredients, but if you need to purchase another one, you can get it within the range of $250 - $500.

- Shelves:

This is the most essential storage unit. It is even more important if you are settling for a home bakery, since you might be starting out in a small kitchen. Shelves are extremely effective in managing your limited space. They will help you store your equipment, utensils, supplies and ingredients properly, in order to keep your workplace neat and free of congestion. Your freshly baked products can cool off on your shelves before packaging. They also make it easier to locate items. Research the kind of shelf that is adequate for the capacity of your business and the available space. A suitable shelf can be bought within the range of $30 - $70.

- Bins:

Of course, bins are essential to trash waste materials, containers and paper bags from ingredients.

- Backup pans and utensils:

It is also necessary to have backup equipment and utensils like pans, bowls and other supplies, in case of an emergency. You can never be prepared for when you get overwhelmed with orders, so it is better to have a surplus of materials, than to have insufficient materials.

Other Supplies and Equipment

Physical Materials

These include aprons, gloves, hair nets or bonnets, hats, footwear, work napkins, and a first aid kit. These production gears are essential to prevent contamination of baked products and keep them as clean as possible. They are also necessary for protecting the baker from burns or other commercial accidents. Also, since you're running an online bakery and a delivery service will be employed, you will need a delivery van or bike. Having a company delivery vehicle will make your business more official and reliable. If you intend to partner with delivery companies, ensure you go for ones that are credible and include the cost for that in your business plan, (McdonaldPaper, 2018).

Packaging

Your packaging is the first material your customers will make contact with when interacting with your product. Your packaging shows your business image. It is necessary to research different packaging ideas and decide which one is most appropriate for the brand you want to sell.

Licensing and Permits

As a food business, your bakery needs appropriate licenses and permits to function legally. The paper work will include insurance forms, tax identification numbers, etc. Do not neglect the local laws of your state or country. Go to the right bodies and ensure your bakery meets the right standards. Settle all mandatory licenses and permits to avoid complications in the future. This can be done by seeking professional support.

Things to Consider Before Buying Bakery Equipment

The cost of setting up a bakery and buying baking equipment is not money you can easily throw around. Therefore, it is important to do research and ensure you're buying the right equipment that is suitable for your bakery. Since you are establishing a home bakery, you might not buy the equipment an industrialized bakery will buy, due to space. Proper research should be done to avoid investing in the wrong bakery equipment.

Quality

As much as it is tempting to cut costs, be sure it is not at the expense of the quality of the equipment. Quality equipment is crucial for the smooth operation of your bakery and ensures anticipated profit generation. If you invest in equipment of low quality, you are going to spend a lot of money making repairs, due to malfunctions, thereby spending more at the end of the day. Purchase equipment that is durable and of high quality. The quality of important equipment like ovens, mixers, refrigerators, etc should not be compromised.

Usage and Maintenance

Is the equipment on your list user friendly and comfortable to use? Are they easy to maintain? Does each piece perform its functions properly? For your equipment to last long enough, maintenance is a necessity.

Business Needs

As a startup home bakery, what are the essential pieces of equipment your business needs?

Whether you have the money or not, it is not prudent to spend money on equipment you do not need. You have to identify the most crucial needs of your bakery and determine the equipment that are fit to meet those needs.

Space

The size of the equipment to be purchased is dependent on the available space in your home kitchen. Ensure to buy only equipment you need at startup, so as not to congest your work environment. Another option is to plan for a good shelving technique that can help you effectively manage space and shelve properly.

Warranty

When purchasing bakery equipment, it is advisable to go for equipment with high and credible warranty. Some new equipment does not offer warranty, so it is important to find out. The length of the warranty also matters. A warranty will give you the opportunity to either repair or replace your equipment if it develops any fault within the warranty period, with the manufacturers bearing the cost of that. Warranty helps you save on repair costs and gives you confidence that you are buying from a trusted company.

Budget Size

The kind of equipment you will buy is also dependent on your budget size. If the prices are significantly higher than your budget allows, you can decide to leave out some equipment that is not a priority and decide to purchase them later. You can also go for less expensive, but quality equipment. Another option is purchasing well maintained used equipment from reputable restaurants. You can also buy from suppliers that sell equipment at wholesale prices and give fair discounts. Some of the suppliers also provide installation, maintenance and repair services.

Advantages of New Bakery Equipment

One major reason bakery owners buy used equipment is to save money. There is no other advantage of buying used bakery equipment. The advantage of purchasing new equipment is that you have warranty on the equipment, as opposed to used equipment which does not offer a warranty. For a product that has a warranty, depending on the number of months, you can always take it back to the supplier when the equipment develops a fault. For used equipment, the repair expenses are not covered. One of the important things to consider when purchasing bakery equipment is durability. You are not just thinking about cutting cost, but long term usage. There is no guarantee that the used equipment will serve your bakery for as long as intended, since they are going to run for several hours each day. With used equipment, there is a higher probability of a breakdown. So, with new equipment, you spend more during purchase and save up money for early repair due to your warranty offer. With used equipment, you spend less during purchase and more during repairs with no warranty offer, leading to revenue loss. Another thing about the warranty offer is that you are not worried about making the wrong repairs because it is the manufacturing company that will handle your repairs, so they know exactly what is wrong with your equipment.

Buying new equipment affords you the opportunity to use recent technology, and since the used equipment has already been used by a bakery for a period of time, they would not have the most recent technology. Recent technology means improved features and greater efficiency. Buying new equipment also gives you the opportunity to choose from a variety of equipment based on your prefered specification, while buying used equipment will have you pick whatever is available. Also, used equipment that develops faults after a short while can be annoying and discouraging to whoever is operating them. Since the used equipment has been used, the efficiency will be very much reduced and they will end up slowing down the work. One of the biggest setbacks of a bakery business is breakdown or malfunctioning of equipment. Buying used bakery equipment is not an entirely bad idea, but it is important that you understand the option you are going for and decide whether cutting your cost for it is really worth it. It is also necessary to understand the advantages of spending that extra little cash to go for new equipment and decide whether it is worth it or not.

Chapter Four: The Business Logistics You'll Need To Take Care Of

Creating A Business Entity

A business entity is an establishment a person (or persons) forms for the purpose of operating a business, performing a trade or a related action. Your business entity determines how your business operates and how it is taxed. You have the opportunity to create any business entity you choose while starting a business. The kind of business entity you will form is dependent on some key factors, such as business activities, number of owners the business has, potential investors, impact of taxation, local and state laws, the liability protection needed, etc. Types of business entities include sole proprietorship, limited liability company (LLC), partnership and corporations. We will dive into a detailed explanation of these entities, to give you an idea on which business entity is fit for your business. The kind of business entity you form will influence the kind of investors you will attract to your business, so it is important to consider your decision carefully.

Sole Proprietorship

In a sole proprietorship, the business and the business owner are one and are not separated from each other. The business owner is called a sole trader or a private entrepreneur. This is the simplest and most common type of business entity. You do not need to draw up agreements or bylaws for its operations. You are also not obligated to file with local and state registers. Notwithstanding, it is advisable to ensure you tick the right boxes before launching a sole proprietorship; have a proper business plan, get a satisfactory and available business name, and brand properly for adequate visibility. A trademark protection is also recommended, if you have thoughts of expanding your business later on. A sole trader can either be self-employed or a tradesman. As a tradesman, a sole trader can employ other people. An example of a sole proprietor is a freelancer, retail shop owner, consultant, etc.

A major issue with the sole proprietorship business entity is that it has less tax advantages than corporations and offers no liability security. It is also difficult to get business loans and funding from investors. The business owner is responsible for any business debt, since the owner is inseparable from their business, and personal assets can be used to clear debts. One way to avoid a crisis like this is to get credible insurance, to cover up for any liability issues.

Partnership

In a partnership, two or more people can come together to own a business and share responsibilities. Whatever decisions are made have to be defined by a partnership agreement. The agreement will specify details on profit and loss shares, ownership percentages and other essential components. In a general partnership, starting capital is not required. The general partners are responsible for all the company's management decisions; they have the right to intervene in ongoing management and also to demand profit gained at whatever point they wish. However, a general partnership might be disadvantaged in terms of liabilities. All partners are accountable for any debt or liability obtained by the company; it doesn't matter if it was caused by only one of the partners. Most people who form partnerships do it to reduce the weight of starting a business alone. However, it is important to choose the right partner to avoid disputes which can limit the growth of your business.

However, there is another option for partnership, which is the limited partnership. This is one way to avoid shared liabilities. In a limited partnership, at least one of the partners is known as the general partner. As the general partner, they are completely accountable for all of the company's liabilities, engagements, as well as management. For a limited partnership, it is advisable to acquire liability insurance. Also, in this type of partnership, at least one of the partners stands in as a silent or limited partner. A silent partner is responsible for their legal shares and has to invest their own cash as initial capital, while it might not be required for the general partner to invest his/her money as initial capital. This silent partner might not be involved in the management and operations of the company, is not responsible for any liabilities and has no right to represent the company without permission from the other partners. A partnership operates like a sole proprietorship in the area of profits and losses, which are conferred to the owners straight from the company.

Limited Liability Company (LLC)

This business entity is very flexible. This business organization is more official and it can be adjusted to fit various functionalities. If an LLC has only one owner, it can be referred to as a disregarded entity, which is very much similar to a sole proprietorship. Just like the sole proprietorship and partnership, profits and losses from the company are conferred directly to the owner. The owner is then responsible for paying taxes. Unlike the sole proprietorship, in a single member limited liability company, the company is regarded as a legal entity, independent of the owner. Therefore, this permits liability protection, thereby ensuring that the owner's personal assets are protected should there be an issue of unsettled company debts or a lawsuit.

Two or more people can come together to form a limited liability company and can choose to either be taxed as a partnership or as a corporation. They can then avoid double taxation and enjoy the limited liability protection provided by corporations. However, there are situations whereby the liability protection can be lost. Whenever there is a liability issue, you have to bring evidence to show that the limited liability company is an independent legal entity from the owner. This will prevent attorneys or creditors from confiscating your personal assets. This evidence can be brought about by ensuring not to use personal assets for business or business assets for personal use, keeping entirely different accounts and finances, and arranging meetings as frequently as possible. Also, the limited liability company should construct an exposited functional agreement on how the company should operate. The functional agreement should also specify the purpose of each member and the ownership percentages. A limited liability company can either be public or private. The administration of the company is controlled by the managing directors, board of directors and a supervisory board, which will be selected by the shareholders. The shareholders will also be in charge of issues concerning distribution of dividends, accounts and personnel, while the duty of the board of directors is to "supervise the managing directors and provide them instructions as to how to fulfil his or her duties towards the company's goals," (Leppävaara 2015).

Corporations

A corporation is a more official business entity. At least three individuals can come together to form a corporation. The owners have shares in the company and are called shareholders. Shareholders are paid via dividends from their shares or they can sell their shares to the company. Although, not all companies pay dividends. Some instead decide to reinvest profits back into the company to foster expansion. A corporation is restricted by the number of shareholders or its size. It must not have several shareholders to attract future investors. Just like a limited liability company, corporations will also choose a board of directors which will stand in for the shareholders and manage the corporation and ensure that every law is complied with. Compared to other types of business entities, a corporation might be more complex and expensive to run because the corporation must have corporate bylaws that govern the affairs of the corporation, its management, officers' responsibilities, rights of shareholders, etc.

How To Choose Which Business Entity Is Fit For Your Business

Your business must fall under one of the types of business entities. It depends on a number of factors and the particular form in which you want your business to operate. The important factors that should influence your choice include tax engagement, liability protection requirements, the functionality of your business, and investor demand. While it is possible to switch between business entities, it is essential you take your time to choose which business entity best suits your business, as the process of changing entitities can get complex, particularly for businesses with plenty of owners or assets. A small business that does not need a high startup capital or that has little investment demand, and is also owned by just one person can operate as a sole proprietorship or a single member limited liability company. The taxes on these business entities are relatively low. Nonetheless, remember that the downside of running a sole proprietorship is that there is no liability protection. If you intend to run your business with a partner, you can form a partnership and acquire insurance for your business. Ensure that you choose a business entity that is low-risk and does not have the potential of running into enormous debts or heavy lawsuits. If you know your business will eventually need liability protection, then it is best to form a limited liability company or a corporation. If your business is required to obtain many assets, if it involves high startup capital or massive investment, or has the potential to run into heavy debts, then a corporation will be best for your business. It will provide stability and a more solid business structure.

Apart from liability protection, the tax engagement should be an important condition. Small businesses should go for sole proprietorships, limited liability companies and partnerships, as they proffer better taxations and tax advantages. Bigger businesses should go for corporations, because despite the larger and double taxation, since they will acquire many assets, they will have liability protection in case any liability issues arise. For the tax engagement of the different entities, you can speak with a tax professional to get more insight. Whatever decision you make, make sure to confer with a lawyer who can thoroughly go over your options, so you can pick the business entity that is best suited for your business.

Steps To Forming A Business Entity

1.   Choose A Business Name:

Choose a business name that is unique and stands out. Verify with your state to ensure that the name is still available and has not been taken by another business. Each state offers a business name directory where you can do a free search. You can also check national records to ensure that the business name has not been taken by someone in another state, to avoid dispute. You can also protect your business name by registering for a federal trademark. Obtaining a trademark will give you an advantage when a legal dispute arises.

2.   Select A Legal Structure:

There are many factors to consider before selecting a legal structure. These factors include investor demand, the needs and functionality of your business, tax involvement, and liability protection requirements. It also depends on your state, as different states provide different benefits and repercussions for the respective legal structures. As stated above, you can choose to form your business entity either as a sole proprietorship, partnership (general or limited), limited liability company, or corporation.

3.   Determine Your Location:

The next step after selecting a legal structure is to determine your location. Determining your location is crucial, because the location of your business influences the kind of laws and regulations applicable to your business. For instance, cottage food laws apply to food companies established at home.

4.   Register Essential Paperwork:

This step is where you register your business with your state. You will need to obtain permits, clearances, certifications and business licenses before you can successfully register your business. You might also be asked to pay registration fees.

5.   Establish Funding And Taxes:

Establishing funding will be dependent on the size of business you are starting and the needs of your business. This involves creating a bank account for your business. For a business that is not a sole proprietorship, business assets and finances should be operated separately from personal assets and finances, to avoid losing your liability protection. It is also necessary to register annual tax returns to report income. Sole proprietors or private entrepreneurs will have to pay self-employment taxes themselves, as their business will not have taxes withheld. Taxes should be paid faithfully to avoid getting into legal troubles. Make sure you also verify the rules of tax payment in your state to know if you are expected to pay taxes at both state and federal levels, (Gass, n.d.).

Law And Regulations to Comply With

Home Bakery Laws

Of course, before deciding to start a home bakery business, you have to ensure that home bakeries are legal in your state or community, to prevent running into trouble with the authorities. Do proper research and verify information before investing your time and money into your home bakery business, as laws guiding the operations of a home bakery differ from state to state. In Colorado, a food safety course has to be completed before opening a home bakery. In Virginia, you cannot sell wholesale home bakery products to retailers. In Tennessee, it is not mandatory to have permits and kitchen inspections, but you must alert customers with display signage. The state of Mississippi allows small-scale home food operations to sell up to $20,000 of products per year. In Florida, home food businesses cannot employ people, including delivery. Arizona does not demand for kitchen inspections. Food from home businesses cannot be sold to grocery stores, restaurants or online in Alabama. This also happens in Hawaii; only direct sales are allowed. In Idaho, a person can operate small-scale food businesses at home and food products can be sold online, by roadside stands, mail delivery, farmers' markets and delivery service, but everything must be done within the state. It is still illegal to operate home food businesses in New Jersey, as the state is yet to pass a cottage food law. In Indiana, home food products can only be sold at roadside stands and farmers' markets within the state, but there is no restriction on how much you can sell. In Connecticut, your food products must be labeled with a particular language and font size (Warrior, n.d.).

Additionally, it is of extreme importance to find out the licenses, certifications and health precautions that are mandatory for your bakery. While some states require you to obtain certain licenses and certifications, some other states do not demand licenses and certifications from small-scale businesses that are covered by cottage food laws.

Cottage Food Laws

Cottage food laws are laws under the Department of Health that govern the production of commercial, low risk foods at home. These low risk foods may include canned foods, bakery products, jam, dry goods, candies, etc. These laws are only applicable to small businesses that can comfortably operate from home, and there is usually a restriction on the amount of revenue your business can bring in while still regarded as legal. With these laws, there is a balance between local business development and food safety concerns. These laws can also restrict the type of foods you can produce, your sales, and the places you can sell your products. Some states still go all the way to give you particular venues where you can make sales. These are places like roadside stands, events, online, etc. You can choose to use these venues or keep your business solely online. Whatever choice you make, be sure to carry out proper research to know which states have restrictions on online and venue based sales and which states do not.

Kitchen Layout Modifications

Depending on your state's laws, you might have to modify your kitchen layout to make it fit for business activities. You need to do proper research and verify the changes and which ones are mandatory or not. Some states make it mandatory to have a three compartment sink, so you might need to install an additional sink. If it is not mandatory, you might just need to get a sink divider to comply with safety laws. You might also need to install hoods and improve your kitchen's ventilation system. Some states may also require that you have separate sections for commercial storage and food production from your personal kitchen section.

HACCP Plan

HACCP stands for Hazard Analysis and Critical Control Points. In every step of food production, there is a tendency for a food safety hazard to be present, which can cause harm to the consumer. Due to this, it is important to create a HACCP plan which will prevent these hazards. The HACCP plan is set up to recognize physical, chemical and biological food safety hazards and come up with a means to prevent them or reduce the risk of hazard. There are seven important steps that constitute a HACCP plan:

1.   Perform A Hazard Analysis:

This is the first step of a HACCP plan. A hazard analysis can be performed by assessing all the stages of production and identifying the possible hazards that are likely to occur during each of the stages. Examine each stage for the occurrence of physical, biological and/or chemical hazards. It could be in the washing of ingredients and utensils, cutting and peeling of foodstuff, rolling and kneading of dough, etc. An example could be using a chopping board and knife to cut different ingredients without washing them. This can cause cross-contamination and the spread of food borne infections.

2.   Define The Critical Control Points:

After identifying the hazards, the next step is to determine the points whereby the hazards can occur. These points are called critical control points (CCP). A critical control point is a point during the food production process where control must be implemented, so as to get rid of or prevent the possible occurrence of food safety hazards. In this step, you will identify particular points in the production process where hazards can be reduced to a safe level. Examples of critical control points are, manipulation of food like rolling or kneading dough, storing or reheating food, delivering of foodstuff from a supplier, delivering food products to customers, etc.

3.   Set Up Critical Limits:

After defining the critical control points, you need to set upper and lower limits to each of those points in your production process. The purpose of setting these limits is to prevent hazards that are likely to occur or to suppress them to a minimal level. These limits establish regulations on food production and food safety. An example of setting up critical limits is setting appropriate temperatures and time for a food process, like cooking meat for 20 minutes at a minimum temperature of 100 degrees Celsius, in order to properly kill bacteria present in the raw meat.

4.   Institute Supervisory Procedures:

After setting up critical limits, you also need to set up procedures to monitor that these limits are in fact implemented. The purpose of instituting these supervisory procedures is to track your production process to detect errors, implement control measures to correct the errors, and document events for future reference. Whenever there is an issue, with supervisory procedures set in place, you can effectively determine at what point something went wrong. An example of this is using a clean thermometer and a stopwatch to monitor the temperature and time of cooking meat.

5.   Set Up Corrective Actions:

Supervisory procedures are set up to track your production process and ensure there is no error. What if an error surfaces? There should be a plan in place for effective crisis management. If a contamination is detected midway through production, effective supervision would ensure that the contaminated product does not get to the customers and the product is properly discarded. Apart from this, it is also important to identify the cause of the contamination (or any other error) and set up a plan to prevent its recurrence. An example is detecting a physical or chemical contaminant inside a batch of dough. That particular batch should be discarded and the source of the contaminants should be traced. It should be ensured that other batches are not also contaminated from the same source.

6.   Test Run Your HACCP Plan And Ensure It Works

It is always necessary to review your plan frequently and make sure it is actually working and helping you to produce safe food products for your customers. Review your hazard analysis and ask: Are there new hazards? Are there steps in your production process that are beginning to produce hazards? If you have improved your production process, like acquiring a new machine or implementing a new dough rolling technique, then you need to review your critical control points. If you identify new critical control points, then you need to establish new critical limits and supervisory procedures and also set up new corrective actions. Reviewing and improving your HACCP plan helps you ascertain the success of your plan to prevent or reduce the occurrence of food safety hazards. An example is a daily review of critical control points and critical limits.

7.   Maintain Proper Records:

The absolute success of your HACCP plan depends largely on this step. Proper record keeping helps you to effectively detect errors and promptly implement corrective actions. You should document critical limits like time and temperature, previous errors, sources of errors, corrective actions taken, delivery items, personnel and dates, suppliers, maintenance and servicing of equipment and dates, etc. For example, recording temperature helps you to detect when there is a deviation from the appropriate temperature, or recording supplies helps to trace a hazard to the supplier that provided it, (WebstaurantStore, 2018).

Health Inspections

It is necessary for your home bakery to undergo certain health inspections, especially since you are operating a bakery in a residential environment. During health inspections, the health officers will evaluate your entire bakery, from your workspace to your equipment, sanitation methods, hygiene practices, ingredients, manner of storage, etc. Health officers may also inspect baked products, if any, and also ensure that your products and ingredients are stored at appropriate temperatures. Health officers carry out health inspections to ascertain that food companies prepare and handle food in accordance with state health regulations to protect the public and prevent the risk of food infections. Ensure that you meet all the health requirements to avoid sanctions on your business, (WebstaurantStore, 2021).

Getting Ready for a Health Inspection

- Reexamine Your HACCP Plan:

An HACCP is one of the most significant aspects in quality control, as it recognizes the crucial points in food production that have the highest risk of food contamination. Identifying these points will help you come up with a plan to control production towards the prevention of contamination. Knowing the kind of business you are running, the health officers may inquire about your HACCP plan and expect the right answers, so it is advisable that you conduct a review and make corrections where necessary.

- Get Acquainted With Health Code Violations:

If you fall victim to any health code violation due to ignorance, that might not be a worthy excuse and you might still get sanctioned. Look out for processes or methods that can cause cross contamination, poor hygiene, inadequate kitchen sanitation, wrong chemical storage, improper storage, and any other thing that can violate health codes. Also look out for TTC (time and temperature control), as inappropriate time and temperature control can give room for harmful bacteria to grow and cause infection. Research the appropriate temperature that each product and ingredient is to be stored to avoid improper food storage. Organize your kitchen properly to avoid improper storage of utensils. Keep a hygienic environment by wearing appropriate personal protective equipment (PPE) and washing your hands as frequently as possible. This will help you develop the habit of ensuring personal hygiene in your bakery. Check for corners in your kitchen or equipment that easily store dirt and clean them regularly to prevent buildup. Finally, chemicals used to clean should not be found near your ingredients or bakery products, (WebstaurantStore, 2020).

- Perform Self Inspections:

Do not wait for external health officers before you inspect your bakery to ensure health safety. The purpose of carrying out health inspections is not just to prevent health code violations or escape sanctions, but to also control food safety hazards and guarantee safe bakery products to your consumers. The things to look out for during a self inspection include:

- **Food Preparation:** Ensure that gloves and properly sanitized hands are used to handle food. The utensils used should be properly cleaned. Food should be heated using appropriate temperatures and time. Frozen food should be thawed correctly under running water or inside a refrigerator. Cross-contamination should be prevented at all stages.

-       **Food Storage:** See to it that food, especially dry ingredients, are stored in a clean and dry place. All materials should be stored in a place that is not subject to contamination. Chemicals should not be stored near food ingredients. Food should be stored with the First In, First Out (FIFO) method, and should be stored at least six inches above the floor.

-       **Sanitation:** Ensure that all utensils are sanitized properly before and after use. Equipment should be cleaned frequently to avoid buildup of dirt. Utensils are covered with protective cases or covers to protect them from dust or other contaminants.

-       **Maintenance of Refrigerator and other equipment:** All food items and ingredients stored in the refrigerator should be properly labeled. Ensure that the thermometer is well visible and functioning properly. All equipment should be frequently serviced and service dates should be properly recorded to ensure effective monitoring.

-        **Disposal of Refuse:** Refuse should be appropriately disposed of and refuse bins should have lids. The refuse area should not be near your workspace and the area should always be kept clean. Refuse should not be allowed to build up and bins should be emptied regularly.

-        **Personal Hygiene:** Personal protective equipment (PPE) should be worn while working to prevent contamination. Hands should be washed as frequently as possible. Eating should not be done in food preparation sections. Clothes and aprons worn should be clean and covered properly. Work shoes should also be worn to protect workers from accidents.

licenses And Certifications Necessary For Starting A Home Bakery

Obtaining the required licenses and certifications for your home bakery is important because they will ensure that things are done legally and ethically. They also serve to protect yourself and the general public, since it is easier to trust bakeries with licenses and permits. So, these requirements are put in place for the health and safety of the consumers. The process of obtaining licenses and certifications is similar in many countries and states, but it is still necessary to carry out further research.

Food Safety Certification

Many states require you to acquire a food safety certificate before you can start your home bakery. These states make state-authorized food safety courses available, as you can learn ways to handle food neatly and appropriately, in order to prevent cross-contamination and avoid transmitting food-borne illness to your baked products.

Local Health Department Registration

This registration is done in your local health department to guarantee that your home bakery business meets the standard health requirements and is safe enough to sell home bakery products to the general public. There are two kinds of permits obtained from this registration: "Class A" and "Class B" permits. With a "Class A" permit, you are permitted to make direct (person to person) sales of home bakery products to customers. This permit allows you to sell these bakery products at farmers' markets, events, roadside stands, market compartments, etc. With a "Class B" permit, you can still make direct sales, as with a "Class A" permit, while also being permitted to make indirect sales to other businesses, like restaurants, cafes, etc. The "Class A" permit costs around $100-150, which is a bit cheaper than the "Class B" permits which goes for around $150-250. A "Class B" permit also involves kitchen inspections. Each permit is required to be renewed annually. Registration of your home bakery business at the local health department will require you to fill important forms and supply sufficient information about your business.

Certification of Acceptability

The state of your food production environment, that is, your home kitchen, is inspected. This inspection is carried out by an environmental health and safety officer. If your home kitchen meets the criteria, the certificate is then conferred to you. The criteria to be met include the cleanliness of your kitchen environment and equipment, existence of satisfactory storage and packaging facilities for ingredients and baked products, waterproof and non-porous kitchen countertops to prevent the absorption of food materials during baking, proper personal protective gears like aprons and hair nets, satisfactory washing facilities, and proper refrigeration, (Lambrechts, n.d.).

Application For licenses And Certifications For A Home Bakery

Obtaining licenses and certifications for your home bakery may vary from state to state. Nevertheless, the steps to obtain them are quite similar:

1.   Look for the municipal office closest to you. This municipal office is where you will be given the necessary forms to obtain your licence. Put a call through, explain the kind of business you intend to run, and get proper information on the required licenses and permits to be obtained.

2.   After getting adequate information, go to the municipal office with proper identification and all other required documents. Go to the health and safety department in the municipal office and follow all the stated rules.

3.   Ask for the essential forms to be filled and fill them out appropriately. After filling out the form, submit it together with your application fee.

4.   Wait patiently for feedback from the health and safety department. An inspection by a health officer will be scheduled to guarantee that your home kitchen is up to specific health standards. You can prepare for the health inspection.

5.   Your licence or permit will be issued to you if your home or kitchen passes the health inspections. The licence is usually mailed to the address of the home bakery or picked up at the health department. It is worthy to note that registration of a home bakery is connected to your address at the time of the registration. This means that if there is a change in location, registration will have to be done again, (Southern States Insurance, 2022).

Resources for More Information

•   Cottage food laws in the United States (Rice et al. 2018)

•   Foragers Cottage Food Community Website (*Cottage Food Laws*, n.d.)

•   Institute for Justice: Cottage Food Laws and Food Freedom Laws (*Recent State Reforms for Homemade Food Businesses*, n.d.)

- Department of Health

- Department of Agriculture

- Chamber of Commerce

- Municipal Centre

- Department of Agriculture's Food Safety Division

Chapter Five: Where to Set the Bar When It Comes to Pricing Products

Determining The Prices For Your Bakery Products

There are several factors to consider when it comes to determining your pricing strategy for your bakery products, so that your business does not run on a loss. While drawing up your business plan, your pricing strategy is one of the things you should discuss while drafting out your marketing plan. This chapter will expand on the pricing strategy and give a breakdown on how to come up with profitable prices for your bakery products. The price of your products is the only marketing element that directly brings income to your business. Therefore, your pricing strategy is of extreme importance. You have to consider both the fixed and the variable costs of production. With proper consideration, you should be able to come up with suitable prices for your products.

How to Set the Right Prices for Your Bakery Products

As a startup home bakery business, you are doing everything; you are managing, baking, marketing, handling customer care and administration, and sometimes even doing deliveries. If all these are not put into consideration, there is a tendency to overwork and not get the monetary value for your work. Even if you have people doing all of these, you would also need to consider wages and hires. This is why it is important to do proper research before starting your business. Draw up a suitable business plan; do not rush, and set up proper prices for your products. Do not be afraid to set prices that are actually worth the value of the products. One of the popular thoughts that comes into the minds of bakers who are starting a small-scale bakery business is that setting high prices will make them lose customers. While it is true that your prices might automatically repel certain people, do not allow the fear of losing customers make you undervalue your products, thereby making you set unprofitable prices. Below are strategies to determine the prices for your bakery products.

Competitor Research

One strategy to setting prices for your products is researching your local successful competitors to discover how much they charge for similar products. Of course, you do not have to adopt the same prices they use, but this research will give you an idea of the price range for your products.

Map Out Sales Expectations

This should also be done while writing the financial plan of your business plan. You need to estimate your sales to give you an idea of how much you hope to earn in one, two or three years. This will help you set your prices efficiently. Your sales expectations can be optimistic, but should also be realistic. Your sales expectations will influence your pricing bracket, preferred target customers, customer insight value, and in turn, the price of your bakery products. Your sales expectations will also help you determine how long it will take for you to pay back your startup costs. Do you want to spend the first two or three years paying back startup costs, or do you want to pay back startup costs and still get profit? All these will influence the price of your products. Factoring in your sales expectation while determining the price of your products will also help you discover whether your sales expectations are too high and help you decide whether to reduce your expectation, reduce your cost of production, or find a way to increase sales while balancing the cost and profit margin.

Study Prospective Customers

Who are your target customers and how much are they willing to pay for your product? If your target customers are people who would rather go for cheap bakery products than expensive ones, then you have no business making expensive products because you will not sell your products consistently. If you want to make expensive products or set your prices higher, then you might have to change your target customers. One of the important factors that determines the price of a product is consumer insight of value. You need to research your target market and find out how much your prospective customers are willing to pay for your products. Are there extras you offer that they are willing to pay for? If not, do you want to remove them or focus on the target customers willing to pay extra? Identify the demographics that are willing to pay higher for your bakery products and the strength of that demographic.

When done properly, this study will help you to identify the price sensitivity of your target market and come up with a discount strategy.

Try Out Premium Pricing

If you produce bakery products of high quality, the prudent thing to do is to set high prices. This particular strategy works best for luxury and premium products, rather than general products, and your target customers will be consumers who are after good quality and are willing to pay for it. You can also set premium prices for products that you either invented, are new to your target market and competitors, or are scarce. These products can come with unique designs, flavors, etc. The moment the product begins to gain popularity in the market, the price can then be reduced gradually, to avoid losing out on competition. This is called "Price Skimming," (Kamari, 2020).

Monitor Your Costs

To set prices that are worth your products and also give you substantial profit, you need to take records of your costs. Monitor your fixed and variable costs, and any extra cost incurred during production. Keep record of the cost of every ingredient, electricity, equipment maintenance, etc. Do not leave out anything. Also, be aware of your overhead costs, as it will help you determine your cost per unit. One effective way to monitor your costs while baking is to use precision baking. The use of precision baking involves the use of weight while handling your ingredients. It helps your recipe be accurate and consistent, and also helps you to calculate the exact amount spent per grams used. Ensure that all the ingredients in your recipe are in ounces, calculate the cost of one ounce based on the total cost of the ingredient, and then multiply the cost by the number of ounces used. This will give you precise figures that, in turn, makes it easy to calculate the price of each product.

Discounting

After calculating your total cost and determining your profit margin, you can also consider making discount sales to attract more customers. You can take advantage of seasons and holidays like Valentine, Summer, Christmas, etc. to give discounts on your products. You can use the "buy two, get one free," technique. Another technique is psychological pricing, when a product is made to look cheaper than it is. You can attract customers by setting a $4 product at $3.97 or $3.99. This makes the product look cheaper when, in fact, it is a very small discount. You can also use the "penetration" technique by launching your products at a discounted entry price. Proper communication with your starting customer base will allow you to increase the prices after launch.

Determine Your Preferred Pricing Bracket

Your target market research should help you decide what pricing bracket you want your bakery business to belong to. Do you want to make high or low-end products? This decision will influence the price of your products.

Consider The Timing

As an independent home business baker, it is easy to ignore timing while running your business. If you are a contracted baker, you will most likely charge hourly rates. This should not be different from your business. While calculating the price of your products, you might just calculate your total cost and profit, without giving much attention to the time you spent. This should not be how you do it. You should monitor how long it takes to bake your products, and set your hourly rate, so as to incorporate it while calculating the price of your products. Considering your time while calculating your price shows how much you value your time. When you do not consider your time while baking, it shows you are only selling your ingredients, not your expertise and time. Setting your hourly rate is dependent on how much you want to pay yourself. Whatever figure you come up with is an interpretation of how much value you place in your work.

Step-By-Step Process For Determining Pricing

If you want to make substantial profit from your home bakery business, then pricing your baked goods requires strategy and confidence. Hence, the key to a thriving bakery business is setting the right prices. Below is a step-by-step process to setting accurate prices for your products:

Step 1: Calculate The Recipe Cost:

Keep a spreadsheet containing the list of ingredients and how much they cost. Your recipe costs include:

- **Ingredients Cost:** Record the quantity of ingredients used for that particular recipe and calculate the cost from the total cost of the ingredient. For example, if you bought a crate of eggs for $3.6 and for that recipe, you used 5 eggs, you need to calculate the cost of those 5 eggs. 1 egg will be $0.12, so multiplying it by 5 will give you $0.6. The same goes for the flour, sugar, flavour, etc. Calculate the cost of each ingredient per batch.

- **Total Recipe Cost:** After calculating the cost for each quantity of ingredient used, sum up the total cost for the recipe. For example, you can sum up the ingredient cost of the flour, butter, sugar, eggs, flavour, milk, decoration cream, etc. and the total recipe cost will yield $12 in this example.

- **Recipe Yield:** How many products/units does your recipe yield. For example, you were able to get 36 cupcakes out of a certain recipe batch. That is your recipe yield.

- **Cost Per Unit:** After summing up your ingredient cost to get your total recipe cost and determining the recipe yield, you can get your cost per unit by dividing the total recipe cost by the recipe yield. For example, if your total recipe cost is $12 and you produce 36 cupcakes from that particular recipe batch, then your cost per unit is

$12/36, which will give you $0.3 to make each cupcake.

Record this cost in your spreadsheet (ingredients cost, total recipe cost, recipe yield and cost per unit), so it can be a standard cost for that particular recipe batch.

Step 2: Calculate Your Time Rate:

First, determine your rate and then record how long it took you to produce that particular product. Your time rate can be determined by how much you think your time is worth. You can always increase your hourly rate, but make sure to start with something realistic. What time did you start baking and what time did you finish? How long did it take you to weigh your ingredients, mix, roll and cut the dough, bake, decorate and package your product? Let's put an estimated time of 2 hours per recipe batch, and let's put a sample hourly rate of $15 per hour. So your time rate is 2 hours multiplied by $15, that is $30 per recipe batch. To get the cost of your labor per recipe unit (remember we have a sample of 36 cupcakes), divide $30 by 36 cupcakes, which will give you $0.8.

Step 3: Factor In Overhead Costs:

Your overhead cost consists of your fixed and variable costs. Record all your fixed and variable costs on the spreadsheet and calculate the cost per unit/product.

-        Fixed Costs: Fixed costs are constant and do not depend on sales quantity, but rather on time. Calculate your fixed costs per month. For the ones paid per year, divide it by 12 months to get the cost per month. For example, overhead fixed costs can be: $30/month for a utility such as water, $10/month for website hosting, etc. Let's assume the monthly overhead fixed cost to be $60. The next step is to calculate the cost per unit by dividing the monthly overhead fixed cost by the estimated number of units produced. Assuming you produce 500 units each month, your fixed cost per unit will be $60/500, which will give $0.12 per unit.

-        Variable Costs: This cost changes with respect to sales quantity and other factors. This includes packaging materials, leasing costs, equipment maintenance, delivery fees, marketing costs, etc. Calculate the cost for packaging 36 cupcakes; either cupcake boxes or cupcake liners.

Also include the cost for branding each product. We can assume the overhead variable cost is $18 per recipe batch, so the cost per unit is $18/36 cupcakes, which will give $0.5 per unit.

Step 4: Calculate The Cost of Goods Sold (Total Cost):

The formula for calculating the cost of goods sold is Recipe Cost per Unit + Time Rate per Unit + Overhead Cost per Unit (Fixed + Variable Costs) = Cost of Goods Sold.

From the above examples:

Recipe Cost per Unit = $0.3

Time Rate per Unit = $0.8

Overhead Cost per Unit (Fixed + Variable Costs) = ($0.12 + $0.5) = $0.62

Therefore, the Cost of Goods Sold (Total Cost) = $0.3 + $0.8 + $0.62 = $1.72 per cupcake

Step 5: Determine Your Profit Margin

A successful business requires getting a solid profit that you can invest back into the business to keep it running. Your profit margin is dependent on your target market. Some bakers set their profit margins as low as 5% because their target customers are cheap buyers. This will yield higher sales and revenue. However, this will only work for general products and not for premium or luxury products, like wedding cakes, or unique recipes. Bakers who set a low profit margin cover up for it by reducing the cost of production, removing certain ingredients or unprofitable items, or even reducing the quality of their products. Your target market can also determine your customer insight of value. How much are your potential customers willing to pay for your products? You can fix your profit margin between 10- 30% of each unit.

Assuming the Profit Margin for your cupcakes is 30% of your Total Cost, it will be $1.72 multiplied by 30/100, which will give you $0.50 per unit.

So your Sales Price will be the Total Cost + Profit Margin, which is $1.72 + $0.50 = $2.20 per unit

If you sell a box of 12 cupcakes, then the Total Sales Price will be $26.40 per box.

Record this in the spreadsheet and compare your price with your competitors. What is the price limit the market will allow? (Grant, 2020).

Importance of Setting the Right Prices For Your Products

•   Setting the right prices for your products will attract the right customers to your business. Your pricing strategy has to go in line with your business plan and perceived target customers. If your prices do not match your customer insight for value, you will not attract your target customers and you will end up attracting the wrong customers.

•   It helps you run a profitable business. You cannot assume your production costs or how much profit your business should get. Assuming your prices or using your competitors prices would not help your business run accurately. For one, your cost of production and overhead costs may be different from theirs. Calculating these things will give a detailed knowledge of your production costs and the most suitable profit margin, thereby helping you to set the right prices for your products. Hence, you are able to make monitored profits from your business.

•   It will help you build good financial habits. Setting the right prices for your bakery products will help you monitor your production costs, thereby making you aware of which items, ingredients or equipment are unnecessary, which products are more profitable and how to adjust your production to fit into your profit margin. It also helps you to reduce waste and know how to maximize and substitute certain items. These financial habits will help your business thrive better.

Chapter Six: How To Get Your Baked Goods To Your Customers

An important aspect of owning a baking business or any business at all, is how to get your goods to your customers. There are a couple of things to figure out, ranging from how customers place their orders, to how to handle the delivery.

In this chapter, we'll walk through how to go about building a website, finding an alternative way to receive orders, and making arrangements for pick-ups or delivery.

How to Receive Orders

There are quite a few options available when it comes to taking your customers' orders. Some of these options include building a website, emails, text messages and DMs on social media.

Building A Website

Today, a company's success depends on its presence online. Online shopping, ordering, and food delivery are all growing in popularity. This is why having a website is a good idea. You can either hire a website designer to build you a website or you can build it yourself.

How to Build a Website for Your Business:

- Pick a Domain Name

A domain name is a website's distinctive address. It typically comprises the name of the website and a top-level domain name, (eg: .gov, .org, .com, etc.).

The proper domain is crucial to the promotion of your company. The name of your bakery combined with a keyword, such as the service you provide (which in this case is a bakery) would make the perfect domain name. Keep it simple, easy-to-remember, and punctuation-free.

Here's a list of websites where you can register your domain name:

1.   NameCheap

2.   BuyDomains

3.   Domain.com

4.   Bluehost

5.   Google Domains

6.   Hover

7.   Dreamhost

8.   GoDaddy

9.   HostGator

10.   Network Solutions

- Pick a backend services provider (Software / CMS "Content Management System")

Without an efficient application handling the backend, it is hard to create a functional website. The part of the website you don't see is called the backend (or "server-side"). Data storage, data organization, and client-side functionality are all responsibilities of the backend. When the frontend and backend are in communication, data is sent and received for a web page to be displayed.

Backend-as-a-Service (BaaS) providers help provide web developers with pre-written software. BaaS vendors offer automation for your backend needs and integrate them with cloud services. Here's a list of BaaS vendors to check out:

1.	Back4App

2.	Firebase

3.	Kinvey

4.	Parse

5.	CloudBoost

6.	Hoodie

7.	AWS Amplify

8.	Bankendless

9.	Kuzzle

10.	Kumulos

● Select a Website Template

You don't need a lot of technical knowledge to build a website. You simply need to pick a template and customize it to your taste. Although they are offered at a much lower price point, you can be confident that the style and build will be of a good grade because they were created by an experienced website designer.

The choices for website layouts are numerous. The first thing you should consider is which platform—the most popular ones being Squarespace, WordPress, Wix, and ShowIt—you feel most at ease with.

● Collect a Number of High Quality Images

In building your website, you're going to need a couple of high quality images. These images can be images of your previous work, or images sourced from the web. You can hire a product photographer to take pictures of your product, so that they are unique to your website.

Finding quality photos for your website online might be more difficult than it seems. You want them to be of the highest quality, pertinent, and duly authorized so that you can utilize them without opening yourself up to legal issues.

Here are websites that offer high quality images:

1.	Unsplash

2.	Pixabay

3.	Pexels

4.	Rawpixel

5.	Canva

6.   Flickr

7.   Wikimedia Commons

8.   Stocksnap

9.   Snappa

10.   Same Energy

Some of these websites offer free images, while some are paid. Make sure to find out the modus operandi of these websites. (Kristy, n.d.)

- Prepare your content

To build a website, you'll need to write some content called website copy. Website copy is the content you display on individual webpages in your website. It is basically what you want to say to your customers through your website.

There is no need for the copy's formula to be very complex. The following are the components of most content blocks:

1.   Headline

2.   Sub-Headline

3.   Image

4.   Block of texts

5.   Call to Action

- Add Webpages

Homepage

The homepage is usually the first page people come across when they open your website. It should contain the main information about your business as well as a picture of your bakery.

You should start by describing your work in detail, who you perform it for, and where you are located (if the location is important to your bakery). Your homepage should also include a Call to Action (CTA) button for the most important action you want your customers to take. For example: "Place an Order" or "Contact Us."

About

It's crucial to establish a personal connection with potential clients by describing who you are and why you are the ideal baker for them. On this page, you can write a story about how the bakery started, or a short bio about yourself, and how your business runs.

You can also include your location, or area of service; any information about your business that you deem important for your customers to know.

Menu

Customers should be made fully aware of the kind of things you sell in order to save both you and their time when they inquire about something you don't provide. This is another justification for listing prices on your website, even if they are just listed as a "Beginning From" price.

Gallery

In the gallery, you can display images of your previous work to motivate customers and to give them an idea of what you can do.

If you offer different types of pastries, you should divide the images into categories. In order to maintain consistency throughout your images, you may keep things simple by placing your cakes and baked goods on a plain background. This way, customers can visualize what their events would look like with your pastries.

Contact

This is one of the most important pages on your website. It is the end point of the entire website. The intention is for everyone to see this page and then contact you to either make an order or arrange a preliminary inquiry. Through the contact page, you can also collect your customers' data for targeted email ads. Your contact page should contain:

- Your address/location
- Mailing address
- Business hours
- Business phone number
- Links to your social media pages.

Ordering Page

There are different ways to take online orders. One of them is to have a dedicated ordering page on your website. Using WordPress or a website building software, you can build an online ordering system and take orders from clients there. Customers place orders directly through the website, and you handle payments, pickups, and orders as they come in.

Review Page

Reading reviews written by previous customers can help build trust. Therefore, you should have a page where customers can write reviews and even post pictures of their purchased goods.

Frequently Asked Questions (FAQs)

If you constantly get asked the same questions by customers, it is a good idea to collate these questions and provide answers to them on your FAQ page. This way, you can reduce the time spent in answering questions from individual customers.

- Test-Run the Website

After adding your web pages and content, it is time to test the website. How functional is it on a computer and a phone? Do the links work? Is the website responsive? Do the images look right? Can customers really place orders and use the contact form?

It is advisable to get someone that doesn't have technical knowledge to test the website. This way, you can see how easy it is for customers to navigate your website. (Harsh, 2021).

Pros and Cons of Building Your Website

Pros

- You get to save money on hiring a professional website developer. Although building a website yourself isn't free, you still get to save money on hiring a professional.

- You have complete control and access to your customer data, which can help with email marketing.

- You get to work at a comfortable pace.

- You'll be aware of what to expect. People who advertise themselves as professional website designers might actually be novices. But, if you're designing the website yourself, you already know your skill level and what you can do. You can even learn new things just to get your desired result.

- You are in the ideal position to build your website because you are the expert on your industry. If you choose the proper designer, they will undoubtedly be familiar with your niche, but they do not represent your company.

Cons

- Building your website yourself means running it yourself in every way. You might not have the technical skills to handle technical difficulties such as a crash or even ordering issues.

- Building a website requires learning a new skill; not enough to become a professional website developer, but enough to build a functional website.

- Making a website on your own is time-intensive. Even when done by a professional, building a website is time intensive. Given that you have little to no experience in website development, it's going to take even longer for you to get a working website together.

- Designers have a working knowledge of SEO (Search Engine Optimization). Even though you may be familiar with the fundamentals, you shouldn't leave this to chance, especially considering the significance of a good search page ranking to your business.

Hiring a Website Developer for Your Business

Usually, the first step to hiring a developer for your website would be to check professional platforms like LinkedIn, Upwork and Fiverr. But getting a developer is one thing, and getting a developer that can make your vision come alive is another.

So, instead of going directly to search for website developers, here's an easier route to take:

● Go through websites in your industry for an hour or two. Then take note of which websites you resonated with and would love yours to look like.

● Reach out to the owners of these websites and find out who created their websites. Some of these businesses might have an in-house developer, but you can still reach out to them to see if they would like to work for you in their free time.

● Reach out to a few business contacts or organizations you are affiliated with in addition to your website list.

●   Obtain the contact information for three to five different designers, then send them a summary of the work you need done and a list of the websites you love and would like to model. (Today's Eggspert, 2021).

Pros and Cons of Hiring a Website Developer

Pros

●   You get a professional website.

●   There's no need to solve problems on your own.

●   You get to relax and just supervise the process.

●   You have a professional that can handle any technical issue.

Cons

●   It can be costly

●   It still requires your feedback and input.

●   You'll always need the developer to take care of issues and updates.

Alternative Methods of Receiving Orders

Not everybody can afford to build a website. In the long term, having and managing a standalone website is a wise investment, but you don't need one to launch your online store. Without a website, there are several methods to connect with your audience, present your pastries, and complete transactions. Here are some quick and easy methods to display and sell your baked goods online without having to spend money or time on a website:

Joining Well-Known E-Commerce Sites

E-commerce sites like Shopify, Amazon and Etsy provide sellers a practical way to sell their products to people around the globe. Although these platforms might be expensive to use, there are many benefits. There might be strict regulation on edible products like who can make, package and sell food. These sites would usually have a seller's guide that contains specific information about selling food items.

Also keep in mind that there is fierce competition on these platforms, so on top of everything else, you probably have to pay for in-platform advertising. In addition to this, you might not be able to stand out among the number of sellers on these platforms. (Navarro, 2021).

Use Ordering Forms

You can simplify your ordering process by simply filling out an order form. You don't necessarily need a website to have an ordering form. Although you can have it on your website too. Having an ordering form can be as simple as having your customers fill out a Google form.

Here are the necessary fields that should be in your ordering form:

- **Bakery Logo:** To make your Google form have a personalized feel, include a logo or banner of your bakery at the top of the page.

- **Customer Name:** Provide a field for the name of the customer.

- **Email Address:** It is important to have your customer's email address, especially if you don't have an integrated payment method and you have to send out invoices.

- **Telephone Number:** Have the customer include their functional phone number in case you need to reach them for any reason. This field should not be optional.

- **Date of Pickup:** It is important to know the delivery or pickup date for every order, so provide a field for pickup date.

- **Time of Pickup:** Customers should also provide the time for pickup, or delivery, as the case may be.

- **Location of Pickup:** This should have a drop down menu of pickup locations you have. For example, if you have affiliated restaurants that you use for pickups, you can add the names of the restaurant, with their address so customers can choose a pickup location close to them.

- **Pastry Type:** If you offer different types of pastries, include them in the menu here.

- **Cake Type:** Give options of cakes you offer for example, chocolate cake, cheesecake, chocolate & vanilla, coconut cake, carrot cake, fruit cake, and vanilla cake. You should also provide a free space for typing other types that aren't on your list if you're open to custom orders.

- This field can be dependent on what the customer chose in the "Pastry Type" field. If the customer picks "Cake", then this field should appear. If not, it shouldn't.

- **Cake Size:** Include an option of the different cake sizes you offer. Provide a free field too.

- **Icing Type:** Include a list of your icing types.

- **Colour:** Provide a field for the customer to fill in the color or combination of colors they want.

- **Words on Cake:** Here the customers get to include the words they want you to write on their cake.

- **Custom Orders:** Customers often want personalized goods, like a cake with a unique design. So, you need to include a field where customers can type details of the cake they want. In addition to this, you can add an optional field for customers to upload pictures of what they want.

- **Direct Message Option:** Optionally, you can include a link to your Whatsapp DM in case customers have encountered any issue while placing their order. If you're not taking orders via Whatsapp, you have to insist that customers fill the Google form to place an order.

- **Payment Method:** You can integrate a payment option if it will work for you. Or simply send your customers their order invoice via email.

(*Bakery Order Form Template*, n.d.)

Take Advantage of Social Media

Sometimes, you don't need to look too far to find what you need. Many small businesses overlook the fact that they already have internet channels that can be used for sales. You can use your different social media apps like Facebook, Instagram and Whatsapp. All you need to do is to create a profile, consistently display your goods, and have customers DM or call to place their order. Some social networking platforms also include cutting-edge, specially designed e-commerce capabilities, for example:

- Marketplace on Facebook

●   Catalogue on WhatsApp

●   Facebook Shops the online storefront on Facebook and Instagram

●   Instagram Shopping

Your ordering process doesn't have to be too formal. It can be as simple as asking customers to DM you to place their orders. You can also provide a link to your Whatsapp chat on your bio. This way, customers can message you directly on Whatsapp to discuss what they want and you can send them your account details for payment.

How to Fill Multiple Orders

As your business expands, it will become increasingly difficult to track orders, if you don't have an efficient system in place. A lot goes into every single order; order taking, production, packaging, and delivery, and it is pretty easy to mix things up.

Orders for baked goods can get complicated because there are so many different flavors, sizes, layers, fillings, icings, and decorations that can be requested. Mixing things up can lead to customer dissatisfaction and can even make you lose money.

Ensuring accuracy is a vital aspect of managing bakery orders. To know exactly what to bake, when to bake it and when to get it to the customer, there are a couple of methods to use.

● **Order Sheets:** Order books come in hard copies and electronic formats. You can even customize your own order sheet or just buy one from Amazon. Even better, you can build an order book using Google Docs, Microsoft Words Sheets or Excel. You can have the customer fill out the order book or do it yourself so you can easily understand what's written there. Be sure to have the customer go through it and verify that the order details are correct. Then, if possible, get their signature.

● **Planners:** Planners usually have built-in calendars in different formats: hourly, daily, weekly or monthly. This way you can keep track of what order is placed, what you're supposed to be working on and when the order should be delivered. A planner would typically allow you to fill in details like:

1.   Customer name

2.   Order placed

3.   Specifics of the order

4.   Ordering method (in case you need to go back to find information about the order)

5.   Time of pickup or delivery

There are a couple of planners you can try out on Amazon.

●   **Physical Boards:** Another option is to use a whiteboard, or any kind of board that suits you. If you want your orders up where you can easily see them and mark them off, then mounting a board in your workspace is a good idea.

You get to write order details and tick them as you complete each step. You can even use thumb tacks or magnets to attach anything you want to cork boards. This can be anything ranging from order details, baking steps, words to be written on the cake, deadline and delivery details.

●   **Digital Calendars:** Another fantastic tool for remembering deadlines and orders is a digital calendar. Google Calendar is one of the most effective options out there. You may alternate between the year, month, week, and day views on your Google Calendars. With the extra benefit and convenience of having all your order details on your mobile phone, you can include all the information you would have otherwise written down in a planner, (Denise, n.d.).

● **Order Management Software:** With an increase in inflow of orders, it becomes increasingly difficult to manage orders even with most alternative methods. This is where order management software can come in handy.

Order management software is an application that tracks sales, orders and delivery, among other things (Keenan, 2021).

You can find a couple of them online, like Veeqo, Orderbot and Brightpearl.

How to Get the Goods to Your Customers

Sending non-perishable goods is one thing, but sending perishable baked goods is on a whole new level. Your top concern as a bakery owner is to deliver baked goods that are undamaged, fresh, and still tasty, to your customers.

In general, you can't take your time in delivering baked goods. You have to get them to the customer as fast as possible. This is because the bulk of freshly produced baked products lose flavour and texture after three days or less.

This means you don't have the luxury of more than two days to deliver your baked goods. Even though express delivery is usually costly, it is worth the money to ensure that customers get their goods in the best state possible. There are two ways to get your goods to your customers: delivery and pickup.

- **Delivery**

Choosing the best shipping company among the numerous options available can occasionally be challenging. Depending on your location, you should have some available options to pick from. For residents of the United States, there are companies like UPS, USPS and FedEx.

No matter what options are available to you, the most important thing is to be sure that they offer special delivery services for baked goods.

It is advisable to try out different companies to see which works best for you. To avoid paying more than required, make sure you verify the charges for each method you use.

While selecting a carrier, you might wish to take customer service into account. While choosing a shipper, you should base your choice on the customer service you feel most comfortable with, (McCauley, n.d.).

Pros

1.   Offering a delivery option helps to increase your sales. Without a delivery option, you would only be able to serve people in a particular radius. Being able to deliver your goods to customers far away opens up a new demographic, and thereby increases sales. According to statistics, 60% of restaurants can expect more sales when they offer online ordering with delivery, (Beambox, 2022).

2.   It provides convenience for customers. People don't mind paying for services as long as they offer maximum convenience. Did you know that 63% of customers prefer the convenience of delivery over dining out with their family? (Beambox, 2022).

3.   You get the ability to outsource delivery. When using a delivery company, you don't have to worry about making the deliveries yourself or having customers come to your home for pickup. It takes the stress and hassle off your shoulders.

Cons

1.   You have no authority over the independent corporation. If the delivery firm's customer service is subpar, this might harm the reputation of your company.

2.   Order-related communication problems might arise, which can negatively affect consumers.

● **Pickup**

An alternative to outsourcing your delivery to logistics companies is offering a pickup option. There are different ways to do this.

1.   Home Pickup: This is where customers come to your home to get their baked goods. You should have already set a pickup date and time beforehand so both parties are on the same page. Also, you have to send the customer your home address so they can locate your residence easily.

2.   Affiliate Stores: If you're not comfortable with customers coming to your house, or it's simply not feasible, you might want to consider having affiliate stores, restaurants or cafes. You can make an agreement with a store owner close to your residence where you can drop off goods for

your customers to pick up. Of course, you still have to be on the same page with the customer regarding the pickup date and time.

3.   Pickup Points: This service, usually referred to as out-of-home delivery, offers greater freedom than home delivery. You can either have a preset location for customers to pickup from or you can decide the pickup location with individual customers. Although the latter can sometimes be more difficult because some customers prioritize their convenience. Of course you have to charge for this service. Pickup locations provide flexibility, diversity, time and money savings, and can help to prevent missed deliveries.

Pros

1.   You don't have to bother about delivering the product to a logistics company.

2.   It allows for more flexibility. You can pick a location that is close to your home or the customer's home, depending on your agreement. Alternatively, you can pick a location that is open both early in the morning and late at night to suit your customer's schedule. Customers also get to choose the time they want to pick up their

packages at pickup locations (you have to be strict with the time if they're picking up from your home). With a pickup service, customers don't have to wait around at home all day waiting for a delivery; they can go about their days with the pickup on their to-do list.

3.   Choice is a crucial factor for consumers. Customers love it when they are presented with options and they get to choose what is most comfortable for them. This not only makes your customers happy, it also gives your business a good reputation.

4.   Eliminates the chance of making unnecessary expenses on delivery. In the event of a repeated unsuccessful delivery, logistics companies sometimes request fines from the seller. The pick-up option ensures that no issue arises that warrants the product being returned, since the customers are in charge of getting their goods.

5.   It helps to prevent missed deliveries. One of the most common issues in logistics is when the delivery person cannot locate the customer's home, and then they have to return the package to the warehouse, increasing the risk of the product going stale, getting damaged, or not getting to the customer in time.

Cons

1. The sole disadvantage of pickup sites is that customers are more likely to hold your company responsible for a poor delivery than the pickup point itself. Therefore, choosing trustworthy partners is essential if you want to provide a high-quality service.

2. With home pickup, you might have to deal with the inconvenience of customers that don't keep to time. They can feel like whatever time they show up will be fine since you run your bakery from home. This can encroach on your personal time.

3. Having customers come to your home can feel like an intrusion. And sometimes, it is simply not feasible to have customers come to your place. In addition to this, it can pose a security threat, (McCauley, n.d.).

Tips to Ensure Smooth Delivery

Because of the nature of baked goods, they require special attention and effort to make sure that they get to the customer in tip-top shape. Here are a few tips to follow:

● Whenever you ship baked goods, ensure you label them as "PERISHABLE." Usually your delivery company should ask if the package is perishable or not, but it's better to be safe than sorry.

● Verify that your customer is aware that you're sending their goods and will be available to receive it.

● Double-check the package's address and make sure it is attached with very strong tape. Both your address and that of your customer should be attached. There is no room for mistakes when it comes to baked goods.

● Make sure you cool your baked goods before shipping them. Baked goods should not go from the oven to the box, trapping in all the heat.

● Keep your products refrigerated before the delivery. Cakes in particular benefit greatly from freezing before shipping. This keeps the products from deteriorating inside their container. Baked goods should be refrigerated for 12 to 24 hours before shipping or pickup. This way the products get to the customer still fresh and moist.

● When transporting the goods, have an extra set of hands in the car to hold the box for you, to prevent it sliding around or even falling. This is especially necessary for cakes.

● Never put your cakes under direct sunlight. Exposing your cake to sunlight will cause the icing to melt.

● Keep your cake on a flat surface while transporting it. The flattest and safest place in your car should be the floor area of your back seat. Not the back seat itself, but the floor.

● Be extremely careful when you drive. Even with your cake on a flat surface, you can still smear the icing if you drive roughly. Even worse, you can have a layered cake tilt to the side, ruining it.

● If you have a hot climate, then it is advisable to have your AC on when transporting goods.

● The more firmly your baked product is packed within the box, the less space it has to wiggle around, lowering the chance of it becoming messy. You can never have too much stuffing in your box.

● Tape the lid of the box or container shut, to ensure that it stays in place. This will work as an added measure of security in case the box or container tries to open during transport.

●	Give the package a little shake. If you hear rattling or shifting, reopen the package and add more stuffing.

(Rotimicakelady, 2016)

Chapter Seven: How To Promote Your Online Bakery Efficiently

How to Market Your Online Bakery Business to Bring in More Customers

Drawing up a business plan, having a target market and producing your goods are not enough to run a successful bakery business. Your prospective customers will not be aware of your business and the goods will not get to them if you do not promote your business. Creative promotions attract the right customers to your business and help to increase your sales. Apart from attracting customers, customers feel appreciated when they are treated properly and the customer service is top-notch. In this chapter, effective marketing strategies will be presented to give you ideas on how to properly market your online bakery business. While focusing on branding and your business logo when starting your business is good, prospective customers focus more on the visibility of your bakery business and the impression your business gives them, in order to earn their business.

Social Media Promotion

One of the most popular and fastest growing means of effective business promotion is via social media. It is basically a necessity for most businesses to have an online presence, and since you want to run an online bakery, having an online presence is of extreme importance. Make sure your bakery business is available and visible on popular social media channels like Twitter, Instagram, Facebook, Pinterest, TikTok, etc. and post consistently every week.

Create A Content Calendar

What works best for online visibility is having a social media calendar. If the only thing you do on your social media pages is sell your products, you would not get the expected attention, no matter how good your product seems. Apart from posting pictures of your products for sale, you can look for ways to engage with your audience by dedicating a day in the week for motivational quotes. You can use trendy hashtags like *#MotivationalMonday*. Social media channels like Instagram and Twitter make it easy to gain visibility via hashtags. When people go through these hashtags, your posts pop up, and if they are engaging enough, your audience will interact with your posts, which thereby adds to the visibility of your business.

Post Engaging Content

You can post "Did you know?" content or trivia questions. You can also attach prizes or rewards to people who answer correctly. In essence, just make your pages fun and easy to interact with. You can use design tools like Canva to create graphics and video content. You can also post video challenges on TikTok or as an Instagram reel. This helps you monitor and measure engagement. There are some video challenges like "The face and the business" that will show the face of the business owner and a little part of the production process. More people will also interact with your business pages when you post tutorials and tips. You can even post video tutorials on YouTube. The idea of this strategy is that you are able to reach not only those who want to buy your products, but also those who are not interested in buying your products. For example, a fellow baker may find your video tutorials and tips useful and share the video. Their audience gets to see your post and interact with your page. This increases your visibility. A lot of cake lovers like to share nice cake pictures, so taking a few photography lessons to capture attractive pictures is also a good idea. High-quality appealing pictures give your customers confidence in your business and they give your business an advantage on picture social media platforms like Instagram.

Paid Promotions

You can also run a paid promotion on social media channels like Facebook and Instagram. These paid promotions will be visible to app users and create more visibility for your business. You can also collaborate with fellow online bakery businesses or pay food bloggers with a large following to help you promote your business.

Use Location Tags

A lot of business owners ignore location tags while selling their products on social media. Posting with location tags on social media helps your products be visible to customers in that location. Social media platforms like Instagram have made it easier for your posts to reach customers within your location. Users can browse through a particular location, and if that location tag has been used on your posts, they will pop up among the results. Also, some users can be looking for a certain product in a certain location and may not know where to search. A simple "Cakes in Virginia" search, for example, will streamline the search to your location and the results will include your products.

Email Marketing

Another fast rising online promotion strategy is email marketing. This is one of the best ways to reach a wide range of customers. There are email marketing platforms with free plans like Mailchimp, Convertkit, Sender, etc. that you can use. These platforms also allow you to schedule and automate emails. You can place a signup form on your website or social media pages where customers can sign up with their emails, or you can introduce mail orders so that customers' email addresses can be saved to a database which you can convert to a mailing list (with their permission). You can send special offers and new product deals to the email addresses of your customers. You can also send fun emails like "Thank God It's Friday" (TGIF) and new month emails. This creates more visibility, as customers get direct notifications of your special offers, unlike if it were just posted on your page. Even if customers do not respond to every special offer you send, seeing these notifications creates an impression and keeps your business relevant in their minds. Ensure you moderate how frequently you send the emails to avoid spamming your customers, (Copadis, n.d.).

Special Offers

Every now and then, there are unique products that trend and attract customers. Apart from the general products you offer, you can study the market to identify these special products, bake them and market them as premium products. Products like these attract people and raise their curiosity. Your premium products make your business stand out from other bakery businesses. For example, you can bake and market gluten-free bakery products as special products. The effect of this strategy is that it attracts people who are not necessarily recurring customers. A person can be searching for gluten-free bakery products and stumble onto your advertisement. What stands out is not your business, but the special offer, especially since other bakery businesses might not be offering gluten-free bakery products. The offer automatically attracts the person, and if they are pleased with the product, they may spread the gospel of your business to other people looking for the same offer. You can also take advantage of festive periods like Mother's Day, Christmas, New Year, Valentine's Day, any other national or religious holidays and even school holidays to bake special products for sales. You can bake love-shaped cakes or special boxes of doughnuts or cupcakes. You can also offer special combo sales like doughnuts and pies, and make it a little cheaper than the individual prices put together. Most consumers are willing to spend more money during these festive periods. Make proper preparation and advertise your special products appropriately.

Hosting Giveaways

Hosting a giveaway once in a while increases your businesses visibility. You can host occasional giveaways, such as Valentine's giveaways, anniversary giveaways, etc. You can set giveaway rules that require participants to share your business pages and invite friends to interact with your post, follow you and share your page. You can give product prizes, like a box of cupcakes or doughnuts, or you can give out equipment to new bakers, like a mixer. You can make it a giveaway challenge where participants can create content, like graphics, creative pictures, essays or videos, and the most qualified or the entry with the highest interaction will take the prize. This will engage the participants, as people value things they create themselves. You can also run a brand collaboration giveaway with a complementary brand, as this will give you access to multiple audiences. You can post a picture with a "the best caption wins" description. You can also run a referral contest, which can produce massive social media engagement. Placing a deadline on your giveaway also helps to give participants a sense of urgency that makes them want to interact with your post, even when there is a reluctance. You can conduct a quiz for people to answer, with a prize being given to the participant with the most correct answers.

Another means of giveaway is hosting a class for people, to teach them a certain baking skill. Those who win your prior giveaways, or answer your quiz questions correctly, can be given free admission to the class. Despite the fact that you are giving away a prize, the sole purpose of this strategy is to widen your audience and give your business more publicity. Make sure the reward has value and is captivating to your audience. After the giveaway, make sure to reach out to the winner immediately, to avoid the accusation of running fake giveaways.

Create a thank you post and hint on future giveaways. The more people interact with your giveaway challenge, the more your business is promoted.

Setting Up A Booth at Baking Conventions or Trade Shows

Another way to promote your business is by attending trade shows and exhibiting your baked goods. Participating in trade shows gives you better proximity to your target customers. You get to meet different people and potential customers, get in-person feedback about your products and you can even land deals with local shop or restaurant owners. Participating in trade shows as a vendor gives your business more visibility and gives you greater credibility. Social media is a great tool in publicity. Your business may have the opportunity to appear on the social media pages of the organizers of the show, thereby giving it more publicity. Planning for a trade show takes a lot of effort, time and resources, but when executed properly, helps you boost your sales and publicity over a short period of time. It is important to plan adequately so as to get a substantial return on your investment.

Draw Up A Budget And Plan

You can not just walk into a trade show unprepared. You need to effectively plan for your appearance. What are your goals for setting up a booth? What do you hope to achieve? Are you participating just for publicity, increase of sales, or do you want to use the opportunity to launch a new product and get customer feedback? How much will it cost to produce the samples and how much does the booth space cost? Record all these expenses and draw up a precise budget. Come up with a strategy. Who are the fellow vendors and competitors, and how do you plan to stand out? Do you have a specific number of clients you hope to attract? All these will aid your business with proper preparation.

Explore Trade Shows Relevant to Your Business

As a home bakery business, you do not want to participate and spend money on a trade show that is not related or relevant to your business and the products you are offering. Imagine participating in a fashion trade show. Of course, the people in attendance will be fashion vendors, enthusiasts and shoppers. Your bakery business will be out of place and the money invested will be wasted. Research upcoming trade shows related to your business and prepare appropriately for them.

Register And Book A Space

When you find a trade show that is relevant to your business and you decide to participate, do not hesitate to register for it. Early registration gives you more location options and gives you the opportunity to pick a location with good exposure and visibility.

Prepare Your Products, Equipment And Marketing Materials

Shop for all your ingredients and double check to ensure nothing is left out. Service your equipment to avoid disappointment or disruption of your exhibition. If you plan to share fliers, products, price lists, survey forms, etc., all these should be planned for and ready on time.

Announce Your Participation

Announce your participation to the public to attract more attendees. You can make a post on your pages across different social media platforms (Instagram, Facebook, Twitter, LinkedIn, etc.) or even send an email to the customers on your mailing list. Be sure to include specific information like available products, location, booth number or area, etc. You can insert a popup on your website that advertises the trade show, so immediately anyone who visits your website or a landing page will be able to pre-book, or at least will know about your participation. You can also explore paid promotions or ask social media influencers for a shout out. The idea is to make potential customers aware of the exhibition and attract people to your booth.

Create A Unique Design for Your Booth

You need a booth that is unique and stands out. Be creative with your design. There will be other bakery businesses participating in the trade show, so you need your booth design to be creative enough to attract customers. Your booth design should be simple, yet trendy enough to catch the eye. No matter how good your products taste, it is what your potential customers see that will attract them to your booth. So, the effort on your design matters as it helps to create a remarkable first impression. You can also display a nice picture of your previous products or delivery. Customers who attend the trade show would also love to take lots of pictures, so if your booth design is appealing enough, it will attract people to your stand.

Have Good Customer Service

Remember you are not just exhibiting to make sales, but to also increase your customer base. Dress nicely and respond nicely to people. Your interaction with customers leaves a lasting impression, so this is of extreme importance.

Include A Unique Feature

Complementary to your booth design should be a unique feature that is not necessarily your product or part of what you are marketing. You can set up live Instagram prints, offer free water or drinks, play music or conduct an engaging video for customer feedback. You can put up a contest and host a fun game for people to win free products or even set aside some products as free samples for tasting. A lot of people will not risk buying new products or flavors they have not tasted or have no idea about. So, samples can be an advantage for your business. Some customers may approach your booth, taste your free samples, be convinced to buy more and even invite their friends.

Be Active Online

As much as the exhibition can keep you busy, it is important to be active online and post updates as the show goes on. You can go live if you have the resources for it or interact with customers and ask for their social media handles to tag them to pictures you post of them. You can also choose to "live tweet" and come up with a special hashtag which customers can tweet while at your booth. This will allow customers to post their experiences with your products and promote your business to their followers. The hashtag makes it easy for you to find their posts and interact with them.

Network With Other Vendors

Since other food businesses will be present at the trade show, it is important to network to give you the opportunity for future collaborations. For example, you can collaborate with drink companies and run discount sales together. The idea of this collaboration is to give awareness to each other's businesses in your different audiences. So, you are indirectly promoting and increasing sales for each other. Also, since a lot of businesses will be active online during the exhibition, networking can help you feature in some of their posts on social media.

Follow-Up With New Customers

Collect contact details (email or/and phone) from the customers you meet and follow up with them immediately. Post the pictures you took and tag them to it. This will increase your online following. Send an appreciation text or email to thank them for showing up at your booth and checking out your business. You can then ask for a rating or feedback for your products or service. Do this before further promotion or advertisement, as it is important to connect with the customers first, (Jacob, 2018).

Leaving Samples With Local Cafes or Coffee Shops to Promote Your Product

Apart from setting up an online store, another solid idea to effectively promote your online bakery business is to drop samples with local cafes, coffee shops or restaurants. Since you are running an online business, the first contact your customers will make with your products is when the products are delivered. Due to previous bad experiences, some customers will be wary of your business if they do not trust you. Dropping off samples of your products in local cafes or coffee shops can help give prospective customers the opportunity to see products before deciding whether or not to buy. Dropping off samples of your products also widens the range of your customer base, as the customers that frequent these cafes, coffee shops or restaurants can have access to your products. You can negotiate with these shops to either buy your products at a discounted rate and resell them, or take a percentage of the sales made. This will help to boost your sales.

Receive And Share Reviews

Reviews are very important in the promotion of one's business. When marketing a product, especially in the online space, most people will prefer to read the reviews of previous customers before deciding to purchase your product. In fact, many buyers will avoid products sold online without reviews, for the fear of being disappointed or scammed. Posting reviews from your customers not only gives prospective customers a reason to trust you, it also lures in people who have previously seen your products, but have been second-guessing their purchase. Posting reviews is one of the best promotion methods you can apply to your business. Below are some ways to make reviews of your products more visible:

Word of Mouth

While delivering your products, try to encourage your customers to drop feedback after tasting your products. Some customers genuinely forget to give feedback, while to others, it is not something they feel obligated to do. Build good relationships with your customers and ask politely for feedback. Word of mouth reviews are a very effective means of business promotion, as it comes from personal experience and can be trusted. Generally, word of mouth promotion is trusted because the customers that share personal reviews do it because they want to, unlike social media influencers that promote businesses because they are paid to. If your customers are pleased enough with your delivered product, they can help to promote your business and refer other customers, thereby automatically increasing your business audience.

Taking Surveys and Posting Reviews

If you don't have the opportunity to ask for feedback directly from your customers, you can opt for surveys. This works best when you have properly engaged your audience on social media, or when you have an active emailing list. Send personal survey forms to your customers' email inbox, asking them to give feedback on your products. Pick out the best reviews, summarize and transform them into content that can be posted on your social media pages. The idea is that as people engage with your social media pages and posts, they get to see reviews from others that will convince them to make a purchase.

Set Up A Google My Business Page

A Google My Business Page puts your business on the map. This increases the visibility of your business, especially on search engines. People can easily access information about your business by just searching your business name. Not only that, they get to leave reviews on your Google My Business page, which will be visible to anyone who comes in contact with your business page. In the case of new customers who are looking for bakeries near them, all they need to do is search, and your bakery business, alongside other bakery businesses will pop up in the local search results. The kind of reviews and ratings you have will determine whether your business will rank high in the results and whether customers will be attracted to your business or not. So, good customer service is of extreme importance. Treat your customers well, so they leave good reviews of your business. Also make sure the information on your Google My Business page, such as phone number, active hours, business address, products pictures, email address, website, etc. are all accurate. You can also upload a price list on the page.

Offer Value

Another way to promote your bakery business is to seek means to add value in people's lives. Paid promotions are good, but if you think about it, many people are not naturally drawn to direct promotions. This is the reason many businesses are advised to employ copywriters that can create enticing and engaging content for your promotions. Another way to attract people to make more sales for your business is by putting out content that helps people. What most businesses do is have a platform that people can learn from and then input their sales promotion at the end. All these increase your brand presence. Below are some ways to offer value that can promote your business.

Have A Blog Section On Your website

Your website should not just be for the sales of your products and placing orders; you can also have a blog section where you post recipes, baking tips, cake style ideas, ingredient alternatives, baking hacks, etc. These kinds of content can attract cake lovers, home bakers, etc. With well-written, search engine optimized content, your content, and in extension, your website will rank high among results when users search on search engines. When people keep reading your content, your website leaves an impression in their minds, thereby promoting your business. Note that it is important to put your sales promotion at the end of each blog post. Even though it is not guaranteed that every person that reads your blog will be convinced to purchase your product, they will become aware of your business and your products. So, whenever they want to purchase any of your products, they can always refer back to your website. If the content you post is valuable enough, the people who read it can also share with others. Social media has made it easier to share information around, so this is an advantage. There are also social media food influencers that are not necessarily content creators, but increase their audience by sharing valuable content on their social pages. Your content can make it to their pages. This does not necessarily divert the audience from your blog, but increases the visibility of your business, with due credit, of course.

Create A YouTube Channel

A lot of people see YouTube as a lifesaver, as it is a reservoir of all kinds of information. People trying to learn a new skill, students who need more explanation on their course topics, people who find it difficult to operate gadgets or need help to repair them, people who need book or movie reviews and home hacks, etc. all go to YouTube. So, if you are looking to increase sales, a good percentage of your potential customers are on YouTube. Nothing beats giving out information that people find valuable. A food business owner can post cooking hacks like "How to boil rice finely." A lot of people definitely know how to boil rice, but many might not be satisfied with the appearance and will be looking for hacks to cook in a way that appears better. Another example is when home bakers have issues with holes appearing on the surface of their cakes after baking, or their bread not rising enough. Posting video content on how to prepare these foods better, will attract potential customers to your YouTube channel. You can also decide to promote your products or business at the middle or end of your videos. Search engines now give priority to well-optimized video content, so this can increase publicity for your business.

Host Free Online Classes

Another way to offer value is by hosting free online classes. New bakers can sign up for your classes and share with fellow bakers. You can offer classes on baking skills, how to start a bakery business, how to adequately price your products, how to effectively run online sales, etc. When your link is shared to others, or when your advertisements are seen, what gets people's attention is the class you are hosting, and since the bakery industry is growing fast, many people will want to sign up. When the decision is made to register for your classes, interested people are either directed to your website or social media pages, so they get to see who is organizing the class, what your business is all about and what products you are selling. Also, since you will be the facilitator of the classes, your bakery business should automatically be an example and reference point. So, as you teach, you can always make reference to your business, thereby promoting your business. This automatically sets your business as a standard in the minds of your students and they can also make reference to your business, thereby indirectly promoting your business by word of mouth. This means that your business branding has to be top-notch, so that your business can fit the image you present. You can also collaborate with fellow bakery business owners who can take the classes with you. These businesses will share the advertisement for the classes to their audience, thereby increasing the reach of your business.

Sponsor Community Programs

This is one method a lot of brands use to promote their business. When people organize programs, shows, or events and the budget is beyond what they can afford, they look for brands to sponsor the program. The brands donate a certain amount of money to the event in exchange for promotion. Some can offer to take care of customized souvenirs, like writing materials, shirts, bags, bottles, gadgets, etc. Most of these souvenirs are customized with the company's name or logo, thereby publicizing the business to those in attendance. You can sponsor local community events with money, while they include your brand in the advertisement, or with souvenirs. You can also decide to share confectioneries that are packaged with branding, since you are running a bakery business. That way, every attendant is able to come in contact with at least one of your products. Also, since most of these souvenirs are valuable items, they can still be used after the event. Imagine people wearing a shirt that carries your business name around, or carrying a bag with your business name to different locations. To that person, the items are valuable and can be used, but to you, your business is being indirectly promoted to everyone who comes in contact with those items, anywhere.

Offer Discount Sales

This is one major way to promote your bakery business and increase visibility and sales of your products. When people want to purchase items, they always look out for discounts. People research businesses with good quality and cheaper prices. That is why competition analysis is very essential during pricing strategy. It is necessary to know the prices that similar successful businesses set for their products, in order to have a competitive advantage. Most times, discounts have more to do with psychology. For example, imagine a product normally goes for $12, both in your business and your competitors' business, and you decide to do a discount sale and set the price at $11.89. Even though the difference is just 11 cents, what people see is the first figure. So, it seems like $12 against $11, the 89 cents is mostly insignificant, unless the customers pay more attention. You can also take advantage of events and holiday seasons to run discount sales, like mid-year sales, Christmas and Valentine sales, etc. These are periods that customers will be willing to buy more of your products during. You can also add more of your product to orders, like adding an extra cupcake to a box of a dozen cupcakes. If other businesses sell a box of 12 cupcakes for $25, adding an extra one for that discounted price will mean they will get 13 cupcakes for $25. When advertising the sales, you can say, "Buy a box of cupcakes and get one cupcake free." The one extra cupcake may be little, but people like free things, so it will automatically attract buyers, and customers would prefer to buy from your business.

Apart from offering free classes, you can also offer premium classes with slashed prices. For example, if you offer a free baking class and people sign up, after the free class, you can set up a premium or advanced class that people would have to pay for. The advanced class can come at discount prices for those who attended the free class. You can also give promo codes to new customers that can be used on your website, to either reduce the prices of a certain number of products they buy, or give them a 'first purchase' free item. When this strategy is well advertised, it attracts customers to your bakery business. Customers can also win coupons that can be used later on while purchasing your products. Offering loyalty programs is also proven to be effective. Monitor your sales and take record of your most frequent customers and send gifts or souvenirs to them. It could be extra products, like a free box of doughnuts with an appreciation note, or home items like a customized mug, bottle, chopping board, spoons, sieves, can openers, bowls, napkins, etc. It could even be wearable items like shirts, caps, bags, etc.

Chapter Eight: Tips For Creating Delicious Baked Goods and Serving Your Customers Well

Tips For Creating Delicious Baked Goods

Even though it is difficult to eliminate mistakes as bakers and business owners, learning how to manoeuvre certain mistakes will save a lot of money. There have been bakery business owners who have previously made their mistakes and shared valuable directions on how to avoid these mistakes. So, it is wise to gain the knowledge shared, in order to improve the outcome of our business. It has been said frequently that baking is a science. Well, baking is both art and science. The art comes with the creativity in creating new recipes, designs and decorations. Science comes with precise preparation. Recipes have 'rules' and 'instructions' you need to follow, because if you do not, you will not get the desired result. Baking is not very difficult when all these rules are followed and the right preparation is applied. Having knowledge about the right preparation tips will eliminate the anxiety of hoping your products do not flop. In this chapter, we will explore different vital tips for creating delicious baked goods.

Temperature is Essential

One of the most important things to pay attention to while baking is temperature. When precise temperatures are written in recipes, they are not just there for fun. Ingredients can require cold rooms or hot temperatures and the specified temperatures should be adhered to. Think about the yeast used to bake bread. Inactivated yeast needs warm water to get active and utilize the sugar to produce carbon dioxide for proper rising of the bread. If you decide to use inactivated yeast to bake, and you don't adhere to the temperature in the recipe, you will bake bread that will not rise. Also, some ovens, even the ones from big brands, do not have accurate temperatures. That is, the actual temperature is sometimes slightly higher or lower than the specified oven temperature. The difference could be 10 degrees or more, which can go unnoticed if not properly monitored, thereby affecting the turnout of your products. The inaccuracy in oven temperature can damage your products and waste time and money spent on ingredients and recipes. To avoid baking with inaccurate temperature, it is important to bake with an oven thermometer. Set it in the middle of your oven to get the accurate temperature. You also need to keep the oven door closed as constant opening and closing can affect the temperature of the oven, which can also affect the products. If you need to check to see if your cake or bread is done, try to do it quickly, so that if it is not done, the baking temperature will still be consistent to continue baking.

Properly Measure/Weigh Your Ingredients

Get all your ingredients ready before you start baking, to avoid missing out on anything. All standard recipes come with measurements, so it is important that these measurements are followed to get desired results. If you ignore the measurements, your product will be inconsistent. It will either come out dry and hard or too soft and soggy. For measurements that require spoons, for instance, 1 tsp of sugar, use spoons designed to measure dry ingredients. For dry ingredient cups, use the spoon and level method. Scooping the ingredients with the cup can sometimes give you 150% of the ingredients. Instead of doing that, scoop the ingredient into the cup with a spoon. Do not tap the cup as it can cause ingredients, like flour, to settle. After scooping the ingredient, level off the top of the measuring cup. For liquid ingredients, use clear liquid measuring cups that have pour spouts and graduations by the side. Every bakery business owner should have a kitchen scale that can be used to weigh ingredients. Measuring cups can also be used to measure dry ingredients, but it is advisable to use a weighing scale, as you may not scoop or level the ingredients properly with the cups. When you use a properly functioning weighing scale, you are sure to measure the exact amount of grams or ounces of flour needed for your cake or bread. Using a weighing scale helps with precision while baking.

Have The Right Butter Consistency

For the majority of bakery products, butter is the starting ingredient in the recipe, so having butter consistency is of extreme importance. Following the recipe accurately is necessary —what temperature is to be applied to butter, what ingredients are to be mixed with the butter, etc. Most times, baking recipes can require three different butter consistencies — melted, softened or chilled. Melted butter can be liquefied using heat and allowed to cool down a bit to a lukewarm temperature. Hot butter can cook eggs in your mixture, if used properly. The most popular butter consistency is softened butter, which requires room temperature. It should be soft enough to press and cool enough to touch. To get a softened butter consistency, bring out the butter and leave it on the counter for an hour before baking. Chilled butter consistency is placed in the freezer or refrigerator. It helps to produce flaky pockets in certain product recipes like biscuits.

Understand Leavening Agents

Baking soda and baking powder are two leavening agents that are commonly used in baking. They are used to make baked products rise. It is worthy to note that these two leavening agents are not interchangeable and cannot be substituted for each other. Baking soda is basic, therefore, needs acidic ingredients to be activated. Baking powder does not need acidic ingredients; it only needs liquid to be activated. So, be careful not to make the mistake of interchanging the leavening agents, like using baking soda in recipes without acidic ingredients.

Follow The Recipe Judiciously

While it is essential to be creative and innovative as a bakery business owner, it is not advisable to over-substitute the ingredients and steps in your recipe. You can substitute ingredients when you are baking for yourself, or for friends and family, but if you are baking to sell the products, then precision is important. It is recommended for business bakers to be a "perfectionist" in their work and follow the recipe to the letter. This is to avoid doing anything that will damage the product or will prevent it from coming out perfectly, thereby wasting time and money invested into the business. Monitor your ingredient stock so you will know when an ingredient is finished. This will help you to not be unaware during the baking process and then have to substitute the finished ingredients with alternatives. If you still insist on substituting, then it should be done at your own risk, instead of at the risk of your business and customer satisfaction.

Packaging, Storing And Transporting Cakes

Products like cakes are better at room temperature. After baking, allow the cake to cool properly before any additional process and do not be in a hurry to either decorate or package. If the cake is not cool enough, it will melt the frosting used for decoration. When you bring out the cake from the oven, leave it to cool inside the pan for about an hour. Decorate your cakes on the day of delivery, as fresh frosting tastes better. If you decide to decorate a day before, you can store it inside the refrigerator, covered. When delivering, use a cake carrier to transport the cake without fear of the frosting being ruined.

Patiently Complete Each Step in Your Recipe

Baking a large quantity of products can be tedious, which might tempt you to cut corners during production. Taking the easy way out just makes the production prone to mistakes. It is better to follow the instructions closely and apply every step, for the duration specified in the recipe. Instructions like "creaming the butter and sugar together until fluffy", "mixing until finely defined", "folding gently", "leaving to sit until the presence of air bubbles" are all important and should be followed.

Use Quality Ingredients And Materials

There are different brands of materials and ingredients being sold. Ensure you get the best brands to have a smooth baking experience. You can find out which ingredients are high quality from fellow bakery business owners, or if you belong to a baking community, you can get the information from there. You don't want to buy an oven that will damage your products with inconsistent temperatures, or butter that will not cream properly. You can also get good brand recommendations from some recipes, as the recipe writer will know what works best for their specific recipe.

Do Not Over-Mix

Over-mixing while baking promotes gluten development, which in turn creates a tough texture. When kneading your dough, be careful not to overwork the dough.

Rotate Pan Halfway Through

Some ovens come with varying temperatures in different sections. In fact, every oven has a hotspot, (Isensee, 2016). The varying temperatures can affect the product and result in some parts of the product being undercooked, overcooked or even burnt. Some recipes come with the instruction to rotate the baking pan 180 degrees halfway through baking. Instead of constantly opening the oven door to rotate the baking pan, you can limit it to the halftime of the baking process. Opening the oven door frequently will lower the baking temperature and affect the products.

Use Parchment Papers or Non-Stick Foil

While baking, you can line your cake or cookie pans with parchment paper or non-stick foil. This helps with easy removal and cleanup. It also helps the batter and dough bake evenly. So, lining your baking pans and sheets will help your products come out better. You can also use silicone mats.

Always Allow the Yeast to Foam

Yeast is added to the dough during the baking process to make it rise. The yeast should be added to lukewarm water to activate it, and then allowed to sit until it foams. The yeast forming process is an essential part of your recipe. Also, ensure that the water is not too hot, as the heat can kill the yeast. If the water is cold, the yeast will not be activated. Add the correct amount of yeast to lukewarm water and a little sugar (depending on the instruction from the recipe). When the mixture begins to produce foam, it shows that the yeast has been activated.

Other baking tips that will help you produce delicious bakery products include:

• Always preheat your oven

• Flour your work surfaces and working materials

• Grease and flour your baking pans and sheets properly

• Use a toothpick to check if the product is done

• Do not overfill your pan. Always leave room for the batter or dough to rise.

• Keep active yeast, buttermilk, nuts, baking powder, etc. inside the freezer for longevity

• Never store products or ingredients warm

• Scrape the side of the bowl while mixing to avoid inconsistency in batter

- Use accurate, recipe-recommended pan sizes

- Bake in the centre of the oven

- Run cold eggs under warm water to get them to room temperature

(Collier, n.d.)

Good Customer Service Tips for Bakery Business

Good customer service helps you retain customers. It is one thing to use strategies to attract customers and it is another thing to develop strategies to retain them. If you do not treat your customers well, they will not return. It is not magic. Customer service is an essential part of running a business successfully. Naturally, people will not forget the good you do for them and they might even recommend your business to others, so they can also experience your good customer service. You also have to think about customer service while drawing up strategies for your competition advantage. Other businesses will want to treat their customers well, so you should not slack in this area. Generally speaking, everyone deserves respect, so that should be your foundational inspiration for good customer service.

Go Personal

Customers feel special when businesses take a genuine interest in them. Note your most frequent customers and build a deeper connection with them. It can be sending appreciation notes, giving gifts or souvenirs, or sending touching emails via your emailing list. Acts of kindness like these always have lasting effects. Create a segment in your mailing list of frequent customers and send them personal emails. Use customers' first names in conversations because it will make the customers feel special. Engage in conversations with them whenever you have the opportunity to make contact. This will help you get certain important information about them. Make their opinions matter too. You can take surveys and implement some of your customers' ideas. Customers also feel good when they see a change they suggested being implemented. Make it known how valuable their patronage is to your business. Most customers are repelled by businesses that do not care about their feelings. Some businesses do not react properly to feedback from customers and do not care if they stop being a customer or not.

Do not be like that. You might have hundreds of customers, but make each person feel like they matter. We have always heard the statement, "Customers are always right." This is not entirely true, as many customers are usually on the wrong side, but the statement just helps you to compose yourself while dealing with customers and helps you deal with even the worst of them when under pressure. Listen to their complaints, review them and make amends. Never disrespect a customer as that is a bad representation for your business. Be the friendly bakery owner and connect with them personally.

Always Deliver Products on Time

One thing most customers cannot stand is a delayed delivery. If you consistently have a habit of delaying deliveries, it leaves a bad impression on your business. Even if you deliver quality products, there will be an effect on customers' experience if delivery is delayed. They may choose to boycott your business because of this. So, this is something you need to be intentional about. If you are delivering products yourself, you need to ensure you are always punctual. It is better to arrive at the address before time and wait for the customer, than to keep them waiting. If you are using the services of a delivery company, you need to ensure you pick companies that will deliver your products punctually. At the end of the day, if there is a problem with the delivery, customers will not hold the delivery company responsible. They will hold you responsible.

Be Consistent With Offering Quality Products

Consistency matters a lot in customer service. Imagine a customer is impressed with the quality of your products and recommends your business to others, then you deliver sub-quality products. The customers who received the sub-quality products will be disappointed with the customer who recommended your business to them. You definitely do not want to treat your customers that way, due to your inconsistency. Be very intentional about producing quality products and producing them consistently. Wherever your business name is heard, let it be known for the quality products it offers. You can't keep painting different impressions about your business and expect to be taken seriously.

Be As Flexible As Possible

As a business owner, being too rigid will make you not listen to feedback. Remember that you are not making your products for yourself, you are making them for the satisfaction of your customers. If you refuse to be flexible, you might be blind to certain flaws in your business and think you are getting everything right. So, customer feedback is extremely important. If they say there is something wrong with your product, listen to them and take it into consideration. Some complaints may be wrong and you must not implement every change suggested, but being flexible enough helps you to make changes when necessary.

Do Not Ignore Challenges

If you have a challenge when dealing with a customer, do not ignore it. Settle it immediately, as unsettled challenges can sometimes be blown out of proportion. Also, ensure that the challenge is settled calmly, with the customer's satisfaction in mind. Good customer service is about a customer's happiness, so even if you know it is a challenge you should not be blamed for, be ready to take responsibility and apologize so that you can have peace between you and your customers. The customer is more likely to remember how you handled the challenge than the challenge itself, (Arcement, 2021).

Importance of Good Customer Service

Customer service can make or break your business. Why? Below is a list of why customer service is important:

•   Good customer service will attract more customers, thereby increasing business revenue.

•   Satisfied customers leave positive reviews and feedback for businesses.

•   People become frequent customers when they are happy and served well by a business.

Chapter Nine: What Changes When You Scale

Scaling A Business

Scaling a business is all about the capability of that business and its capacity to accommodate growth systematically, infrastructurally, economically, etc. How well can your company handle growth? Growth to a small business can be a blessing or a curse. Will your small business have the capacity to have an increased customer base and delivery capacity, sufficient staff, etc. or will it crumble or take a hit due to an inability to manage these things, thereby having unsatisfactory service and unhappy customers? This is where scaling your business comes in. You need to prepare for the growth of your business, unless you want your business to remain small. Scaling your business helps you to position your business in a way that supports its growth. It will require proper planning, funding, employment of new staff and modifying systems, (Campbell, 2019).

Growing Your Business Vs. Scaling Your Business

Scaling a business and growing a business are two different things, even though they are often mixed up and used interchangeably. Growing a business is centred towards increasing revenue, which most times will end up increasing costs, while scaling a business is centred towards managing growth in a way whereby there is increased revenue and the increased costs will not cancel out the increased revenue. This leads to more growth. So, scaling a business has more to do with managing and sustaining the growth of a business.

Major Signs to Look Out for Before Scaling

- Inability to handle the workload: This is when the workload becomes too much and it might be a struggle handling it. If there are increased orders and the production process becomes more tedious, tendencies such not delivering on time could arise. Even if you still get to finish production on time, there is a limit to the amount of people you can deliver to at a certain period of time. You will observe that you might begin to turn down orders and say you are fully booked. If you keep disappointing your customers, you will begin to lose them. Scaling is needed at this point to manage the growth that increases the workload.

•	As a small business, you might have achieved your short-term goals, but your long-term goals might look far-fetched and unattainable. This may be as a result of not having the right resources or capability to implement the goals. This is a sign to scale your business to accommodate your long-term goals, (Sajid, 2021).

The Pros And Cons of Scaling Your Business

Pros

Business Growth

Scaling your business gives it the opportunity to grow. Your growth will lead to success, which will attract qualified specialists to join your team. It will also allow for technological improvements which will better the functionality of your business.

Increase of General Performance

Scaling helps you review critical areas in the business, implement changes and sustain growth. This automatically increases the general performance of your business. Your intensiveness on automated integration systems like digital and email marketing, CRM, etc. will reduce cost, save time and effort and increase productivity, thereby increasing the general performance. This will, in turn, automatically improve customer experience.

Benefits from Economies of Scale

Economies of scale is an important means of increasing your physical performance in your local target market. This means an increase in production rate, which will reduce the amount you spend on the production process. As efficiency increases, production costs decrease.

Cons

Additional Expenses

Scaling your business requires extra resources, which requires enough funding, so there will definitely be expenses incurred in your business. As much as you may try to manage your growth to reduce costs, it may get complicated at some point due to unrealistic ideas, overestimated successes and your customers not accepting your changes. This might lead to unexpected or unrecovered expenses.

Issues With Workflow

Scale means more hands, which means employment or dealing with more people. People management skills are the most sought after skills in business management. You may have the right ideas, plans and implementations, but if the people employed do not implement them properly, there will be an issue with the workflow. Learn people management skills and study your employees to understand their strengths and weaknesses, and the kind of roles to delegate to them. Also, trust their input and feedback, and do not try to shut down their ideas. You do not need to involve yourself in everything or every conflict or issue. It is important to share proper responsibilities to develop accountability.

Facing Failure

The more a business grows or has potential to grow, the bigger it becomes. The bigger a business is, the more prone it is to fail or get stuck. Scaling your business is a big risk. A lot of small businesses would rather not take the risk and remain small because of the fear of failure. You will need to attend to more orders and deliveries from customers, more production, etc. The work just gets more intense. If your plan is not implemented properly, there is a tendency to get stuck, lose sales and fail to meet long-term goals.

Not Having A Competitive Advantage Over Bigger Companies

As a small bakery business, there are bigger bakery companies doing exactly what your business does. If you decide to scale your business, even if you have a competitive advantage over fellow small bakery business owners, increasing your business capacity means meeting bigger competitors. Bigger companies would already have experience, tools and systems that you are just being introduced to. It might be difficult to create a competitive advantage. Look for ways to stand out in the market and not necessarily 'outdo' your competitors. It may take some time to build a competitive advantage, but just make sure you focus on key areas that will help you run a successful business, (Sapozhnykov, 2021).

How Does Scaling Affect Your Online Home Bakery Business?

Scaling up a home bakery business is not for the faint-hearted. You need to re-strategize your business plan, review your baking processes and systems, and acquire equipment. It may also involve rebranding and re-designing. You will also need to consider a change in food safety standards, since your business is now working on a larger scale. The reason many small-scale businesses choose to remain small is that scaling up makes you deal with a different set of competitors. Large bakery companies have a lot of resources, staff and have penetrated the market, so you will have to do a lot to compete with them. This will include hiring staff, reviewing your baking processes and penetrating a larger target market. Your larger competitors may already have departments in charge of process review, food safety regulations, recipe scale-up, production management, etc. At the point you decide to scale up, if it is just you handling all of these things, it can get discouraging. That is why it is important to carefully research, take the necessary steps and contract necessary professionals that can assist in scaling up your home bakery business. Below are the important changes to note while scaling up a home bakery business.

Change of Venue And Bigger Equipment

Business growth means you will have increased orders and customers. This will require you to acquire bigger equipment. For example, the mixer and oven you are using in your home may not handle the increased capacity of production. You will need to get a bigger weighing scale, bigger bowls, bigger work tables, etc. Now, getting this equipment may present a bigger problem – space. Your home kitchen will not be conducive to a proper working environment, if you need to scale up. You would also have to consider the space when you hire staff. You would not want to work in a cramped up kitchen, as it can slow down productivity. You can set up a ghost or commercial kitchen to handle production better. Also, remember that you registered your business as a home bakery, which means it is under cottage laws. Changing venues and exceeding annual sales limits, due to increased orders, will require re-registration. Commercial bakery regulations will begin to apply to your business. You will also need to obtain extra licenses, permits and certifications.

Recipe Scale-Up

Increased orders can make you sacrifice quality which, in the long run, makes you lose customers. People will always be drawn towards quality, so be careful not to compromise it. Recipe scale-up is not just about multiplying the ingredients. Some ingredients tend to react a different way when they are in higher amounts. They may give off a different texture or taste; they might not fit into your current production process, so you have to review; and there may also be a change in baking time. A change in the quality of your products can affect the shelf-life of your products and make them spoil easily. If the issue is an increased baking time, then you need to carry out thermal profiling to determine the actual baking time. This is very essential, as overbaking can dry up the moisture in your products, making it easily go stale. If the issue is your equipment, consider getting better equipment that can handle the increased output of your production. Contact a professional who will look into your current recipe, the magnitude of your increased production, and help you scale-up your recipe properly, in a way that does not affect the quality of your products.

Organization Structure

When scaling up your bakery business, organizational structure is extremely important. At the inception of your business, you are most likely responsible for almost everything, but as your business begins to grow, handling everything will be catastrophic. At this point, you need to consider hiring staff. You need to move from Founder mode to CEO mode. In a proper business, is the CEO responsible for everything? Founder mode is a state where the founder is reluctant to allow other people to step up and take up responsibilities. The major concern for a founder is cash flow and being able to sort out bills, decisions in the business are made for short-term success and there are strategic long-term goals. Proceeding with this mode will make you lose your creative energy and lead to burn out. The first set of staff to hire are production planners and bakers. The production planner identifies possible problems, decides the most suitable solutions and ensures that the planned production is constantly followed. Below are the detailed roles of a production planner:

•	Ensuring seamless flow of production.

•	Reducing production cost and investment by proper estimation and increase in production efficiency.

•	Ensuring that adequate quality and quantity of ingredients and equipment are being used.

•	Building better communication and understanding with the suppliers.

•	Planning processes and systems to ensure that production is done in the most economical way.

•	Calculating and predicting future data by analyzing past data; that is, monitoring orders and production units per yield to prevent extra cost of storage or waste.

•	Scheduling orders for delivery and ensuring a regular and timely delivery.

•	Creating and improving product designs.

When your production increases and you hire a production planner, it will be unrealistic and draining to handle the production all by yourself. This is why hiring production bakers is important. Production bakers are people who manufacture your products. For a start, you can hire two to three bakers, depending on your increased output. You can choose to hire more if you offer different products and you want each baker to handle a specific product, depending on their skills. You can also hire more if you want to run shifts, especially if you need bakers to work at night to sort out early morning orders.

All this is about getting the right people to do the right job and control the right processes, which helps to strengthen your organizational structure. This, in turn, frees up your time, which you can then use to strategize, lead the company properly, and focus on sales and growth projections, thereby increasing efficiencies and productivity.

Food Safety Regulations

Scaling up requires you to review your HACCP plan and identify new critical control points and safety hazards. Getting a commercial or ghost kitchen and getting new equipment will require a health inspection. You can contact a food safety audit company to inspect your equipment and facilities, and monitor your production process, before a health inspection is carried out by government officials. This will help you avoid health violations. Food safety audits help to raise the standard of the food safety and quality of your products, and also help you improve your sanitation practices. Your workers should not wear earrings and accessories that can contaminate your products; pans with carbon deposits, due to prolonged usage, should be cleaned with a decarbonator; baskets with heavy flour deposits should be cleaned and sanitized; etc.

As your business grows, your production volume increases, which also implies an increase in flour usage. If there is no flour re-cleaning system in place, the flour can cloud the air and get trapped in the air filtration system. With no regular cleaning, this will promote the growth and spread of microorganisms and mould spores. Also, if there is a separate room for packaging, the room has to be completely dry and devoid of moisture. The presence of moisture can also promote microbial growth and contaminate your products during packaging. A proper food safety audit will prepare your business to attain an SQF (Safety Quality Food) certification.

Rebranding And Messaging

As your bakery business is scaling up, you are reaching a bigger market, new customers and bigger competitors. You need to make sure that your brand message is reaching the right people to ensure productive conversion. While scaling up, hire professional brand specialists to look into your business and identify what needs to be improved or changed. Clean up your logo and designs, identify unique features of your business and bring them to life through packaging. You can also consider in-store merchandising that can help create a personality for your business that customers can interact with. This personality should amplify the central purpose of your business and what it cares about, (Coronel & Rucker, n.d.).

References

Arcement, B. (2021). *It's all about serving your customers*. The Business Journals. https://www.bizjournals.com/bizjournals/how-to/marketing/2021/04/it-s-all-about-serving-your-customers.html

Bakery Order Form Template. (n.d.). Forms.App. Retrieved August 1, 2022, from https://forms.app/en/templates/bakery-order-form-template#

Beambox. (2022). *Food Delivery Service Statistics That You Need to Know*. Beambox. https://beambox.com/food-delivery-service-statistics

Campbell, A. (2019). *How to Scale a Business*. SCORE. https://www.score.org/blog/how-scale-business

Collier, S. (n.d.). *100 Best Baking Tips and Tricks*. A Spicy Perspective. Retrieved July 21, 2022, from https://www.aspicyperspective.com/100-best-baking-tips-and-tricks/

Copadis, A. (n.d.). *Bakery Marketing Ideas: 14 Ways to Get More Customers*. Wishpond Blog.

Retrieved July 16, 2022, from https://blog.wishpond.com/post/115675437944/bakery-marketing

Coronel, P., & Rucker, B. (n.d.). *12 dos and don'ts when scaling up food production.* CRB. Retrieved July 23, 2022, from https://www.crbgroup.com/insights/scaling-food-production

Cottage Food Laws. (n.d.). Forrager. Retrieved July 11, 2022, from https://forrager.com/laws/

Denise. (n.d.). *How Do Bakers Keep Track Of Orders And Due Dates?* Whisk Warrior. Retrieved August 1, 2022, from https://whiskwarrior.com/how-do-bakers-keep-track-of-orders-and-due-dates/

Dhliwayo S, Van Vuuren JJ (2007). *The strategic entrepreneurial thinking imperative. Acta Commercii, 7:123-134 - Google Search.* (n.d.). Retrieved June 28, 2022, from https://www.google.com/search?q=Dhliwayo+S%2C+Van+Vuuren+JJ+(2007).+The+strategic+entrepreneurial+thinking+imperative.+Acta+Commercii%2C+7%3A123-134&oq=Dhliwayo+S%2C+Van+Vuuren+JJ+(2007).+The+strategic+entrepreneurial+thinking+imperative.+Acta+Commercii%2C+7%3A123-

134&aqs=chrome..69i57.1956j0j7&sourceid=chrome&ie=UTF-8

Emerson, A., Gunaratne, A., Hebblethwaite, D., & Paulose, A. (2011). *The Drivers of Entrepreneurship in Indian Migrants to New Zealand. An enquiry into the personal, labour market and economic factors promoting entrepreneurial* https://researchbank.ac.nz/handle/10652/2243

Gass, D. (n.d.). *The Complete Guide to Forming a Business Entity in 6 Steps*. Anderson. Retrieved July 11, 2022, from https://andersonadvisors.com/the-complete-guide-forming-business-entity-6-steps-get-started/

Grant, A. (2020). *Pricing Baked Goods: How to Do It the Right Way*. Better Baker Club. https://betterbakerclub.com/pricing-baked-goods-how-to-do-it-the-right-way/

Harsh, L. (2021). *How to Build a Bakery Website*. Sav. https://blog.sav.com/how-to-build-a-bakery-website

Isensee, N.-K. (2016). *15 Tips and Tricks to Improve Your Baking Routine*. Foodal.

https://foodal.com/knowledge/baking/tips-tricks-improve-baking/

Jacob, A. (2018). *A Comprehensive Guide to Exhibiting at Trade Shows for Food and Beverage Wholesalers*. Ordermentum. https://www.ordermentum.com/blog/a-comprehensive-guide-to-exhibiting-at-trade-shows-for-food-and-beverage-wholesalers

Kamari, M. (2020). *6 Pricing Strategies You Can Use When Pricing Your Baked Products*. Amari Baking Centre. https://amaribakery.com/2020/08/12/6-pricing-strategies-you-can-use-when-pricing-your-baked-products/

Katie, B. (2018). *Every Time*. The Work. https://thework.com/2018/10/every-time-your-mind-shifts/

Keenan, M. (2021). *Order Management System: Definition and Best Software*. Shopifyplus. https://www.shopify.com.ng/enterprise/order-management-system-oms

Kotler, P., & GarryArmstrong. (2008). *Principles of Marketing*. 488. Pearson Education

Kristy. (n.d.). *How to get a website for your home baking business*. Bake This Happen. Retrieved August 1, 2022, from https://www.bakethishappen.com/blog/how-to-get-a-website-for-your-baking-business

LaMarco, N. (2019). *List of Items Needed to Start a Small Bakery*. Chron. https://smallbusiness.chron.com/list-items-needed-start-small-bakery-21051.html

Lambrechts, A. (n.d.-a). *14 Tools You Need to Start a Home Bakery*. Philosophy Of Yum Blog. Retrieved July 1, 2022, from https://philosophyofyum.com/home-bakery-tools-appliances/

Lambrechts, A. (n.d.-b). *Home Bakery Business Certificates, licenses and Insurance*. Philosophy Of Yum Blog. Retrieved July 11, 2022, from https://philosophyofyum.com/home-bakery-certificate-and-license/

Leppävaara, L. (2015). *Business Plan For Online Bakery Concept*. https://www.theseus.fi/bitstream/handle/10024/103256/Thesis final version.pdf?sequence=1

Lynch, M., Kamovich, U. (2017). The Language of successful entrepreneurs: an empirical starting point for the entrepreneurial mindset. *Books.Google.Com*. Retrieved June 22, 2022, from https://books.google.com/books?hl=en&lr=&id=74k9DwAAQBAJ&oi=fnd&pg=PA384&dq=mindset+of+business+successful+owners&ots=RlFfSCuhK4&sig=k8ljG1V2k4MQt2K7YSUIGtFzQ3g

Maxwell, J. C. (1998). *The 21 Irrefutable Laws of Leadership*. Thomas Nelson.

McCauley, C. (n.d.). *How to Ship Baked Goods: A Comprehensive Guide*. WebstaurantStore. Retrieved August 1, 2022, from https://www.webstaurantstore.com/blog/3838/how-to-ship-baked-goods.html#choose

McdonaldPaper. (2018). *A 12-Point Checklist of Small Bakery Equipment*. McdonaldPaper. https://mcdonaldpaper.com/blog/small-bakery-equipment-checklist

McGrath RG, M. I. (2012). The entrepreneurial mindset profile of South African small medium and micro enterprises (SMMEs) in the Cape Metropole. *Academicjournals.Org*, 6(15), 5383–5388. https://doi.org/10.5897/AJBM11.2417

Miller, L. (2018). *5 Limiting Beliefs With the Power to Kill Your Business in the Next 12 Months*.

Entrepreneur.
https://www.entrepreneur.com/article/310171

Navarro, T. (2021). *How to Sell Online Without a Website*. LinkedIn.
https://www.linkedin.com/pulse/how-sell-online-without-website-tal-navarro/

PKF Muller. (2016). *Managing Your Business through a Crisis: 6 Steps to Success*. PKF Mueller.
https://www.pkfmueller.com/newsletters/managing-business-crisis-6-steps-success

Recent State Reforms for Homemade Food Businesses. (n.d.). Institute for Justice. Retrieved July 11, 2022, from https://ij.org/legislative-advocacy/state-reforms-for-cottage-food-and-food-freedom-laws/

Rice, C., Leib, E. B., Baikus, O., Hensley, C., Hoover, A., Jerrett, M., Leamy, N., Malavey, M., Smith, L., & Taylor, P. (2018). *Cottage Food Laws in the United States*.

Rotimicakelady. (2016). *9 Essential tips on How to Transport and Deliver your Cakes*. Baking Business School.
https://bakingbusinessschool.com.ng/2016/08/24/9-essential-tips-on-how-to-transport-and-deliver-your-cakes/

Sajid, A. (2021). *Scaling a Business: Effectively Scale Your Business in 2020*. Cloudways. https://www.cloudways.com/blog/scaling-a-business/

Sapozhnykov, V. (2021). *10 Advantages and Disadvantages of Scaling the Business*. Adloonix. https://adloonix.com/10-Advantages-and-Disadvantages-of-Scaling-the-Business-Adloonix

Slater, S. F., & Narver, J. C. (2000). The Positive Effect of a Market Orientation on Business Profitability: A Balanced Replication. *Journal of Business Research, 48*(1), 69–73. https://doi.org/10.1016/S0148-2963(98)00077-0

Southern States Insurance. (2022). *How Can I Obtain licenses, Permits, And Insurance For A Home Bakery?* Southern States Insurance. https://southernstatesinsurance.com/how-can-i-obtain-licenses-permits-and-insurance-for-a-home-bakery/

Today's Eggspert. (2021). *5 Easy Steps To Hire A Website Designer*. CrazyEgg. https://www.crazyegg.com/blog/how-to-hire-website-designer/

Warrior, W. (n.d.). *How to Start a Legal Home Bakery*. Whisk Warrior. Retrieved July 11, 2022, from https://whiskwarrior.com/how-to-start-a-legal-home-bakery/

WebstaurantStore. (2018). *HACCP Plan and Training (With Examples)*. WebstaurantStore. https://www.webstaurantstore.com/article/15/haccp-training.html

WebstaurantStore. (2020). *7 Health Code Violations in Restaurants & How to Avoid Them*. WebstaurantStore. https://www.webstaurantstore.com/article/549/common-restaurant-health-code-violations.html

WebstaurantStore. (2021). *Starting a Home Bakery: Laws, Certifications, Costs, & Marketing*. https://www.webstaurantstore.com/article/43/how-to-start-a-home-bakery.html